SAY IT IN
SERBO - CROATIAN

by Vasa D. Mihailovich
Professor of Slavic Languages and Literature
University of North Carolina

DOVER PUBLICATIONS, INC.
New York

Published in Canada by General Publishing Company, Ltd., 30 Lesmill Road, Don Mills, Toronto, Ontario.
Published in the United Kingdom by Constable and Company, Ltd., 10 Orange Street, London WC2H 7EG.

Say It in Serbo-Croatian is a new work, first published by Dover Publications, Inc., in 1987.

This volume in the Dover *Say It* series was prepared under the editorial supervision of Margalit Fox.

Special thanks to Dr. Radmila Gorup for editing the Serbo-Croatian material and preparing the index.

Manufactured in the United States of America
Dover Publications, Inc., 31 East 2nd Street, Mineola, N. Y. 11501

Library of Congress Cataloging-in-Publication Data

Mihailovich, Vasa D.
Say it in Serbo-Croatian.

(Dover "say it" series)
Includes index.
1. Serbo-Croatian language — Conversation and phrasebooks — English. I. Title.
PG1238.M53 1986 491.8′283421 83-6371
ISBN 0-486-25261-2

TABLE OF CONTENTS

INTRODUCTION

The Serbo-Croatian language belongs to the South Slavic group of Slavic languages together with Bulgarian, Macedonian and Slovene. Serbo-Croatian is spoken by about three-fourths of the Yugoslav population and understood almost everywhere in Yugoslavia. Although some prefer to regard it as two different languages, Serbian and Croatian, it is basically one language with two variants displaying only minor grammatical differences though with substantial differences in vocabulary. These two variants are the Eastern, spoken by the Serbs, and the Western, spoken mainly by the Croats. A major difference between the Eastern and the Western variants occurs in a very large number of words that have an *e* in the Eastern variant and a corresponding *je* or *ije* in the Western, as in *levo* (E) vs. *lijevo* (W) "left" (direction) and *gde* (E) vs. *gdje* (W) "where." The Eastern variant normally uses the Cyrillic alphabet, as Russian does; the Western uses the Latin alphabet. The Latin alphabet, however, may be found in use everywhere and is used in the present book, although the grammatical forms and vocabulary of the Eastern variant have been preferred.

NOTES ON THE USE OF THIS BOOK

The words, phrases and sentences in this book have been selected to provide for the communication needs of the traveler or foreign resident in Yugoslavia, and they have been divided into sections corresponding to the situations likely to be encountered in travel and daily life. Those sections which consist of vocabulary lists, such as "Auto: Parts of the Car" and "Gift and Souvenir List," have been alphabetized according to their English entries. However, the sections on food and public notices have been alphabetized according to the Serbo-Croatian entries to facilitate reference to menus and signs.

The index at the back of the book serves as a handy English–Serbo-Croatian glossary, and helps you to locate quickly a specific word or phrase. With the aid of the index or a bilingual dictionary, many of the sentence patterns included here can be adapted to answer innumerable needs. For example, the place occupied by "six" in the sentence

I'll wait for your call until [six] o'clock

may be filled with another number in accordance with your needs.

In other sentences, the words in square brackets can be replaced with the substitutions immediately following. (These substitutions appear either as bracketed words in the first sentence, or as the indented entries below the first sentence.) Thus, the entry

These things [to the left] [to the right] belong to me

provides the two sentences: "These things to the left belong to me" and "These things to the right belong to me." Three sentences are provided by the following entries:

What do you charge [per hour]?
—per kilometer.
—per day.

The substitutions taken from within a single entry or from the indented entries following a sentence will always be in the correct grammatical form. Since Serbo-Croatian nouns, articles, adjectives and verbs take a variety of endings depending on their context, the substitutions you supply yourself from the index or a bilingual dictionary may not always be in the correct form. However, Yugoslavs should have no trouble understanding what you mean.

As mentioned earlier, the Eastern variant of Serbo-Croatian has been preferred throughout the text. The Western vocabulary variants, where necessary, are indicated with "W" in parentheses. Feminine forms are marked with "F" in parentheses where the main sentence presents the masculine form.

Please note that while brackets always indicate the possibility of substitution, parentheses have been used to provide additional information. They are also used to indicate synonyms or alternative usage for an entry:

Have a seat (OR: Won't you sit down?).

Parentheses may also be used to explain the nuances of a word or phrase or a special usage. The abbreviation "LIT." is used when a literal translation of a Serbo-Croatian phrase or sentence is given in parentheses.

You will notice that the word for "please" has been omitted from many of the sentences of this book (as it has been, for example, in "Have a seat," above). To be polite, you should add the expression "molim vas" *(MO-leem vas)* wherever you would normally say "please" in English.

PRONUNCIATION

CONSONANTS

Serbo-Croatian Letter	*Transcription*	*Remarks*
c	ts	as in ca*ts*
č	ch	as in *ch*ur*ch*
ć	t^y *	as in *t*une pronounced the British way. (A soft palatal sound similar to *ch*. Set your tongue to pronounce *y* as in *y*es and in that position pronounce *t*.)
d	d	as in *d*a*d*
dj	d^y *	as in di*d* *y*ou. (Set your tongue to pronounce *y* as in *y*es and in that position pronounce *d*.)
dž	dzh	as in *j*ob

* Note that in our transcription raised *y* never represents an independent sound. The combination of *t, d, l* or *n* with a raised *y* represents a single palatal consonant.

Serbo-Croatian Letter	*Transcription*	*Remarks*
f	f	as in *f*ine
g	g	as in *g*o (never as in giant)
h	h	as in *h*ill* (pronounced even when at the end of a word)
j	*y*	as in *y*es
k	k	as in s*k*ip In Serbo-Croatian *k*, *p* and *t* are always pronounced without aspiration (puff of air)
l	l	as in *l*et
lj	l^y †	as in pavi*li*on
m	m	*m*other
n	n	as in *n*ou*n*
nj	n^y †	as in ca*ny*on

* Do not confuse this *h* with the letter h used in transcription combinations *ch*, *sh*, *zh* and *dzh*.

† See footnote on preceding page.

Serbo-Croatian Letter	*Transcription*	*Remarks*
p	p	as in s*p*in
r	r	as in *r*un, but rolled with tip of tongue
s	s	as in *s*et
š	sh	as in *sh*e
t	t	as in s*t*ay
v	v	as in *v*ery
z	z	as in *z*one
ž	zh	as in plea*su*re

VOWELS

a	a	as in f*a*ther
e	e	as in p*e*t
i	ee	as in *ee*l
o	o	as in l*aw*, but cut short
u	oo	as in b*oo*t

VOWELS

Serbo-Croatian Letter	*Transcription*	*Remarks*
aj*	a‿ee	as in t*ie*
ej*	ey	as in th*ey*
ij*	eey	as in *ea*r
oj*	oy	as in b*oy*
uj*	oo‿ee	as in ph*ooey*, pronounced as one syllable
r	ŭr	In Serbo-Croatian, *r* functions as a vowel (1) between two consonants and (2) at the beginning of a word before a consonant. Examples: prvi *(PŬR-vee)* "first" and rdja *(ŬR-d^{y}a)* "rust."

* Combinations of a vowel with a following *j* are similar, though not identical in pronunciation to the English diphthongs in the corresponding key words above. In Serbo-Croatian, each component of these vowels is pronounced separately (e.g., *a‿ee* for *aj*), unlike in English, where they are often slurred together.

Serbo-Croatian vowels are never reduced but always pronounced fully. In combinations such as *ae, ao, ou,* etc. each vowel is pronounced separately: trin*ea*st (*TREE-na-est*) "thirteen," im*ao (EE-ma-o)* "he had" and n*au*ka (*NA-oo-ka*) "science."

Throughout the transcription, the Serbo-Croatian words are divided into syllables and the stressed syllable is printed in capital letters.

THE CYRILLIC ALPHABET

As discussed in the Introduction, Serbo-Croatian is written with the Latin alphabet in the Western part of Yugoslavia and with the Cyrillic (or Russian) alphabet in the Eastern part. The Latin alphabet is used throughout this book. The Cyrillic letters and their Latin equivalents are given below so that you may learn to read signs, menus and other notices in the Eastern part of Yugoslavia.

LATIN		CYRILLIC	
A	a	А	а
B	b	Б	б
C	c	Ц	ц
Č	č	Ч	ч
Ć	ć	Ћ	ћ
D	d	Д	д
Dž	dž	Џ	џ
Dj	dj	Ђ	ђ
E	e	Е	е
F	f	Ф	ф
G	g	Г	г
H	h	Х	х
I	i	И	и
J	j	Ј	ј
K	k	К	к
L	l	Л	л

LATIN		CYRILLIC	
Lj	lj	Љ	љ
M	m	М	м
N	n	Н	н
Nj	nj	Њ	њ
O	o	О	о
P	p	П	п
R	r	Р	р
S	s	С	с
Š	š	Ш	ш
T	t	Т	т
U	u	У	у
V	v	В	в
Z	z	З	з
Ž	ž	Ж	ж

EVERYDAY PHRASES

1. Hello (OR: **Hi**). Zdravo. *ZDRA-vo.*

2. Good morning. Dobro jutro. *DO-bro YOO-tro.*

3. Good day (OR: **Good afternoon**). Dobar dan. *DO-bar dan.*

4. Good evening. Dobro veče. *DO-bro VE-che.*

5. Good night. Laku noć. *LA-koo not*^{y}.

6. Welcome. Dobro došli. *DO-bro DO-shlee.*

7. Goodbye. Zbogom. *ZBO-gom.*

8. See you later. Do vidjenja. *do vee-D*^{y}*E-n*^{y}*a.*

9. Yes. Da. *da.*

10. No. Ne. *ne.*

11. Perhaps (OR: **Maybe**). Možda. *MOZH-da.*

12. Please. Molim. *MO-leem.*

13. Allow me. Dozvolite. *do-ZVO-lee-te.*

14. Excuse me. Izvinite. *ee-ZVEE-nee-te.*

15. Thanks [very much]. [Najlepše] hvala. *[NA‿EE-lep-she] HVA-la.*

16. You're welcome. (OR: **Don't mention it**). Nema na čemu. *NE-ma na CHE-mu.*

17. It doesn't matter (OR: **Never mind**). Ne mari. *ne MA-ree.*

18. Don't bother (LIT.: **It's not important**). Nije važno. *NEE-ye VAZH-no.*

19. I'm sorry. Žao mi je. *ZHA-o mee ye.*

20. You've been [very kind]. Vi ste [vrlo ljubazni]. *vee ste [VŬR-lo L^{y}OO-baz-nee].*

21. — very helpful (LIT.: **You've helped me a lot**). — mi mnogo pomogli. *— mee MNO-go PO-mo-glee.*

22. Come in. Slobodno (OR: Udjite). *SLO-bod-no (*OR: *OO-d^{y}ee-te).*

23. Come here. Dodjite ovamo. *DO-d^{y}ee-te o-VA-mo.*

24. Come with me. Podjite sa mnom. *PO-d^{y}ee-te sa mnom.*

25. Come back later. Dodjite opet kasnije. *DO-d^{y}ee-te O-pet KA-snee-ye.*

26. Come early. Dodjite rano. *DO-d^{y}ee-te RA-no.*

27. Wait a minute. Pričekajte minut. *PREE-che-ka‿ee-te MEE-noot.*

28. Wait for us. Čekajte nas. *CHE-ka‿ee-te nas.*

29. Not yet. Još ne. *yosh ne.*

30. Not now. Ne sada. *ne SA-da.*

31. Listen! Čujte (OR: Slušajte)! *CHOO‿EE-te (*OR: *SLOO-sha‿ee-te)!*

32. Look out! Pazite! *PA-zee-te!*

33. Be careful! Budite pažljivi! *BOO-dee-te PAZH-l^{y}ee-vee!*

SOCIAL PHRASES

34. May I introduce [Mrs. Marković?]
Mogu li da vam predstavim [gospodju Marković]?
MO-goo lee da vam PRED-sta-veem [GO-spo-d^{y}oo MAR-ko-veet^y]?

35. —Miss Kostić. —gospodjicu Kostić.
—GO-spo-d^{y}ee-tsoo KO-steet^y.

36. —Mr. Popović. —gospodina Popovića.
—go-SPO-dee-na PO-po-vee-t^{y}a.

37. Pleased to meet you. Drago mi je (OR: Milo mi je).
*DRA-go mee ye (*OR: *MEE-lo mee ye).*

38. How are you? (OR: **How do you do?**) Kako ste?
KA-ko ste?

39. Very well, thanks, and you? Vrlo dobro, hvala, a vi?
VŬR-lo DO-bro, HVA-la, a vee?

40. How are things? Kako je? *KA-ko je?*

41. All right (OR: **Fine**). U redu (OR: Dobro).
*oo RE-doo (*OR: *DO-bro).*

42. So, so. Tako, tako. *TA-ko, TA-ko.*

43. What's new? Šta ima novo? *shta EE-ma NO-vo?*

44. Have a seat (OR: **Won't you sit down?**).
Sedite. *SE-dee-te.*

45. It's a pleasure to see you again.
Drago mi je što vas opet vidim.
DRA-go mee ye shto vas O-pet VEE-deem.

46. Congratulations. Čestitam. *che-STEE-tam.*

47. All the best. Sve najbolje (OR: najlepše).
*sve NA‿EE-bo-l^{y}e (*OR: *NA‿EE-lep-she).*

48. I like you very much.
Mnogo mi se svidjate (OR: dopadate).
MNO-go mee se SVEE-d'a-te (OR: *DO-pa-da-te*).

49. I love you. Volim te (OR: vas). *VO-leem te* (OR: *vas*).

50. May I see you again? Da li mogu opet da vas vidim?
da lee MO-goo O-pet da vas VEE-deem?

51. Let's make a date for next week (LIT.: **Can we meet again next week?**).
Da li možemo opet da se nadjemo iduće nedelje?
da lee MO-zhe-mo O-pet da se NA-d'e-mo EE-doo-t'e NE-de-l'e?

52. I've enjoyed myself very much.
Bilo mi je vrlo prijatno.
BEE-lo mee ye VŬR-lo PREE-yat-no.

53. Give my regards to [your boyfriend].
Pozdravi [svog dečka].
POZ-dra-vee [svog DECH-ka].

54. —your girlfriend. —svoju devojku.
—SVO-yoo DE-voy-koo.

See also "Family."

BASIC QUESTIONS

55. What? Šta? *shta?*

56. What did you say? Šta ste rekli? *shta ste REK-lee?*

57. What's [that] [this]? Šta je [to] [ovo]?
shta ye [to] [O-vo]?

58. What must I do? Šta moram da uradim?
shta MO-ram da OO-ra-deem?

59. What do you want? Šta želite? *shta ZHE-lee-te?*

60. When? Kada (OR: Kad)? *KA-da* (OR: *kad)?*

61. When does it [leave]? Kada [odlazi]? *KA-da [OD-la-zee]?*

62. —arrive. —dolazi. *—DO-la-zee.*

63. —begin. —počinje. *—PO-chee-n^{y}e.*

64. —end. —se završava. *—se za-VŬR-sha-va.*

65. Where? Gde? *gde?*

66. Where is it? Gde je to? *gde ye to?*

67. Why? Zašto? *ZA-shto?*

68. How? Kako? *KA-ko?*

69. How long? Koliko dugo? *ko-LEE-ko DOO-go?*

70. How far? Koliko daleko? *ko-LEE-ko da-LE-ko?*

71. How much? (OR: **How many?**) Koliko? *ko-LEE-ko?*

72. How do you do it? Kako vi to radite? *KA-ko vee to RA-dee-te?*

73. How does it work? Kako to radi? *KA-ko to RA-dee?*

74. Who? Ko? *ko?*

75. Who are you? Ko ste vi? *ko ste vee?*

76. Who is [that boy]? Ko je [taj dečak]? *ko ye [ta‿ee DE-chak]?*

77. —that girl. —ta devojka. *—ta DE-voy-ka.*

78. —that little girl. —ta devojčica. *—ta de-VOY-chee-tsa.*

79. —that young man. —taj mladić. *ta‿ee MLA-deet^y.*

80. —this man. —ovaj čovek. —*O-va‿ee CHO-vek.*

81. —this woman. —ova žena. —*O-va ZHE-na.*

82. Am I [on time]?
Da li sam došao (F: došla) [na vreme]?
da lee sam DO-sha-o (F: *DO-shla*) [na VRE-me]?

83. —early. —rano. —*RA-no.*

84. —late. —kasno. —*KA-sno.*

TALKING ABOUT YOURSELF

85. What's your name? Kako se zovete?
KA-ko se ZO-ve-te?

86. I'm Mr. (OR: **Mrs., Miss**) Ilić.
Zovem se (OR: Ja sam) gospodin (OR: gospodja, gospodjica) Ilić.
ZO-vem se (OR: *ya sam) go-SPO-deen* (OR: *GO-spo-d'a, GO-spo-d'ee-tsa) EE-leet'.*

87. My name is [Ivo]. Zovem se [Ivo].
ZO-vem se [EE-vo].

88. I'm [25] years old. Meni je [dvadeset pet] godina.
ME-nee ye [DVA-de-set pet] GO-dee-na.

89. I'm [an American citizen].
Ja sam [američki državljanin (F: američka državljanka)].
ya sam [a-ME-reech-kee dŭr-ZHAV-l'a-neen (F: *a-ME-reech-ka dŭr-ZHAV-l'an-ka)].*

90. My address is [10 Takovska Street].
Moja adresa je [Takovska ulica broj deset].
MO-ya a-DRE-sa ye [TA-kov-ska OO-lee-tsa broy DE-set].

91. I'm [a grade school student].
Ja sam [učenik (F: učenica)].
ya sam [OO-che-neek (F: *OO-che-nee-tsa)].*

92. — a college student. — student (F: studentkinja).
— *STOO-dent* (F: *stoo-DENT-kee-n^{y}a).*

93. — an elementary school teacher.
— učitelj (F: učiteljica).
— *OO-chee-TE-l^y* (F: *oo-chee-TE-l^{y}ee-tsa).*

94. — a college (OR: **a high school) teacher.**
— profesor. — *PRO-fe-sor.*

95. — a businessman. — biznismen.
— *BEEZ-nees-men.*

96. What is your job (OR: **What do you do)?**
Šta ste po profesiji (OR: Šta radite)?
shta ste po pro-FE-see-yee (OR: *shta RA-dee-te)?*

97. I'm a friend of [Peter Jovanović].
Ja sam prijatelj (F: prijateljica) [Petra Jovanovića].
ya sam PREE-ya-tel^y (F: *pree-ya-TE-l^{y}ee-tsa) [PE-tra yo-VA-no-vee-t^{y}a].*

98. He works for [People's Bank].
On radi u [Narodnoj banci].
on RA-dee oo [NA-rod-noy BAN-tsee].

99. I'm here [on (an annual) vacation].
Ovde sam [na godišnjem odmoru].
OV-de sam [na GO-deesh-n^{y}em OD-mo-roo].

100. — on business. — poslovno. — *PO-slov-no.*

101. I've been here [one week].
Ovde sam [nedelju dana].
OV-de sam [NE-de-l^{y}oo DA-na].

102. We plan to stay here until [Friday].
Planiramo da ostanemo ovde do [petka].
PLA-nee-ra-mo da O-sta-ne-mo OV-de do [PET-ka].

103. I'm travelling to [Belgrade]. Putujem u Beograd. *POO-too-yem oo be-O-grad.*

104. I'm in a hurry. Žurim se. *ZHOO-reem se.*

105. I'm [cold]. [Hladno] mi je. *[HLAD-no] mee ye.*

106. —warm. Toplo —. *TO-plo —.*

107. I'm [hungry]. [Gladan (F: Gladna)] sam. *[GLA-dan (F: GLA-dna)] sam.*

108. —thirsty. Žedan (F: Žedna) —. *ZHE-dan* (F: *ZHE-dna) —.*

109. —busy. Zauzet (F: Zauzeta) —. *ZA-oo-zet* (F: *ZA-oo-ze-ta) —.*

110. —tired. Umoran (F: Umorna) —. *OO-mo-ran* (F: *OO-mor-na) —.*

111. —disappointed. Razočaran (F: Razočarana) —. *ra-ZO-cha-ran* (F: *ra-ZO-cha-ra-na) —.*

112. I'm glad. Radujem se (OR: Drago mi je). *RA-doo-yem se* (OR: *DRA-go mee ye).*

113. I can't do it. Ne mogu to da uradim. *ne MO-goo to da oo-RA-deem.*

114. We're [happy]. Mi smo [srećni]. *mee smo [SRET^y-nee].*

115. —unhappy. —nesrećni. *—NE-sret^y-nee].*

116. —angry. —ljuti. *—L^{y}OO-tee.*

MAKING YOURSELF UNDERSTOOD

117. Do you speak [English]? Govorite li [engleski]? *GO-vo-ree-te lee [EN-gle-skee]?*

118. Where is [English] spoken?
Gde se govori [engleski]?
gde se GO-vo-ree [EN-gle-skee]?

119. Does anyone here speak [French]?
Da li neko ovde govori [francuski]?
da lee NE-ko OV-de GO-vo-ree [FRAN-tsu-skee]?

120. I read only [Italian]. Čitam samo [italijanski].
CHEE-tam SA-mo [ee-ta-LEE-yan-skee].

121. I speak a little [German]. Govorim malo [nemački].
GO-vo-reem MA-lo [NE-mach-kee].

122. Speak more slowly. Govorite malo sporije.
GO-vo-ree-te MA-lo SPO-ree-ye.

123. I [don't] understand. [Ne] razumem.
[ne] ra-ZOO-mem.

124. Do you understand me? Da li me razumete?
da lee me ra-ZOO-me-te?

125. I [don't] know. [Ne] znam. *[ne] znam.*

126. I think so. Tako mislim. *TA-ko MEE-sleem.*

127. Repeat it. Ponovite. *po-NO-vee-te.*

128. Write it down. Zapišite. *za-PEE-shee-te.*

129. Answer "yes" or "no." Odgovorite "da" ili "ne."
od-go-VO-ree-te "da" EE-lee "ne."

130. You're right. U pravu ste. *oo PRA-voo ste.*

131. You're wrong. Niste u pravu.
NEE-ste oo PRA-voo.

132. What does [this word] mean? Šta znači [ova reč]?
shta ZNA-chee [O-va rech]?

133. How do you say ["pencil"] in Serbo-Croatian?
Kako se kaže ["pencil"] na srpsko-hrvatskom?
KA-ko se KA-zhe ["pencil"] na SŬRP-sko-HŬR-vat-skom?

134. How do you spell that? Kako se to piše?
KA-ko se to PEE-she?

DIFFICULTIES AND MISUNDERSTANDINGS

135. Where is [the American Embassy]?
Gde je [američka ambasada]?
gde ye [a-ME-reech-ka am-ba-SA-da]?

136. — the police station. — stanica milicije.
— STA-nee-tsa mee-LEE-tsee-ye.

137. — the lost-and-found office.
— biro za nadjene stvari.
— BEE-ro za NA-d'e-ne STVA-ree.

138. I want to talk to [the manager].
Želim da govorim sa šefom (OR: direktorom).
ZHE-leem da GO-vo-reem sa SHE-fom (OR: *DEE-rek-to-rom).*

139. — your superior. — vašim pretpostavljenim.
— VA-sheem pret-PO-stav-l'e-neem.

140. Can you help me? Možete li mi pomoći?
MO-zhe-te lee mee po-MO-t'ee?

141. Can you tell me how to get there?
Možete li mi reći kako da stignem tamo?
MO-zhe-te lee mee RE-t'ee KA-ko da STEEG-nem TA-mo?

142. I'm looking for my friend. Tražim svog prijatelja.
TRA-zheem svog PREE-ya-te-l'a.

143. I'm lost.
Zalutao (F: Zalutala) sam (OR:Izgubio [F: Izgubila] sam se).
za-LOO-ta-o (F: *za-LOO-ta-la) sam* (OR: *eez-GOO-bee-o* [F: *eez-GOO-bee-la] sam se).*

144. I can't find [the address].
Ne mogu da nadjem [adresu].
ne MO-goo da NA-d^{y}em [a-DRE-soo].

145. She has lost [her handbag].
Ona je izgubila [svoju tašnu].
O-na ye eez-GOO-bee-la [SVO-yoo TA-shnoo].

146. We forgot [our keys]. Zaboravili smo [ključeve].
za-BO-ra-vee-lee smo [KL^{y}OO-che-ve].

147. We missed [the train]. Izgubili smo [voz (W: vlak)].
*eez-GOO-bee-lee smo [voz (*W: *vlak)].*

148. It's not my fault.
Nije moja krivica (OR: Nisam ja kriv).
*NEE-ye MO-ya kree-VEE-tsa (*OR: *NEE-sam ya kreev).*

149. I don't remember [the name]. Ne sećam se [imena].
ne SE-t^{y}am se [EE-me-na].

150. What happened (OR: **What's wrong)?**
Šta se dogodilo? *shta se do-GO-dee-lo?*

151. What's the matter? U čemu je stvar?
oo CHE-moo ye stvar?

152. What shall I do? Šta da radim? *shta da RA-deem?*

153. Leave us alone! Ostavi nas na miru!
O-sta-vee nas na MEE-roo!

154. Go away! Gubi se (OR: Odlazi)!
*GOO-bee se (*OR: *OD-la-zee)!*

155. Help! U pomoć! *oo PO-mot^{y}!*

156. Police! Milicija! *mee-LEE-tsee-ya!*

157. Thief (OR: **Stop thief**)**!** Lopov (OR: Držte lopova)!
*LO-pov (*OR: *DŬR-zhte LO-po-va)!*

158. Fire! Požar (OR: Vatra)! *PO-zhar (*OR: *VA-tra)!*

159. Look out! Pazite! *PA-zee-te!*

160. This is an emergency. Hitno! *HEET-no!*

CUSTOMS

161. Where is the customs office?
Gde je carina? *gde ye TSA-ree-na?*

162. Here is [our baggage].
Ovo je [naš prtljag]. *O-vo ye [nash PŬRT-lʸag].*

163. — my passport. — moj pasoš. *— moy PA-sosh.*

164. — my identification card.
— moja lična karta. *— MO-ya LEECH-na KAR-ta.*

165. — my health certificate. — lekarska potvrda.
— LE-kar-ska POT-vŭr-da.

166. — my visitor's visa. — moja viza.
— MO-ya VEE-za.

167. I'm in transit.
Ja sam na proputovanju (OR: Ja sam u tranzitu).
ya sam na pro-poo-to-VA-nʸoo (OR: *ya sam oo TRAN-zee-too).*

168. [The bags] over there are mine.
One [torbe] tamo su moje.
O-ne [TOR-be] TA-mo soo MO-ye.

169. Must I open everything? Moram li sve da otvorim?
MO-ram lee sve da O-tvo-reem?

170. I can't open [the trunk].
Ne mogu da otvorim [gepek].
ne MO-goo da O-tvo-reem [GE-pek].

171. There's nothing here but [clothing].
Nema ovde ništa osim [odeće].
NE-ma OV-de NEE-shta O-seem [O-de-t^{y}*e].*

172. I have nothing to declare.
Nemam ništa za carinjenje.
NE-mam NEE-shta za tsa-REE-n^{y}*e-n*^{y}*e.*

173. Everything is for my personal use.
Sve je za moju ličnu upotrebu.
sve ye za MO-yoo LEECH-noo OO-po-tre-boo.

174. I bought [this necklace] in the United States.
Kupila sam [ovu ogrlicu] u Sjedinjenim Državama.
KOO-pee-la sam [O-voo O-gŭr-lee-tsoo] oo s^{y}*e-DEE-n*^{y}*e-neem DŬR-zha-va-ma.*

175. These are [gifts]. Ovo su [pokloni].
O-vo soo [PO-klo-nee].

176. This is all I have. Ovo je sve što imam.
O-vo ye sve shto EE-mam.

177. Must duty be paid on [these things]?
Moram li da platim carinu za [ove stvari]?
MO-ram lee da PLA-teem TSA-ree-noo za [O-ve STVA-ree]?

178. Are you finished? Jeste li gotovi?
YE-ste lee GO-to-vee?

BAGGAGE

179. Where can we check our luggage through to [New York]?
Gde možemo da predamo naš prtljag direktno za [Njujork]?
gde MO-zhe-mo da PRE-da-mo nash PŬRT-l^{y}ag dee-REKT-no za [N^{y}OO-york]?

180. These things [to the left] [to the right] belong to me.
Ove stvari [levo] [desno] pripadaju meni.
O-ve STVA-ree [LE-vo] [DE-sno] PREE-pa-da-yoo ME-nee.

181. I can't find all my baggage.
Ne mogu da nadjem sav moj prtljag.
ne MO-goo da NA-d^{y}em sav moy PŬRT-ljag.

182. One of [my packages] is missing.
Jedan od [mojih paketa] nedostaje.
YE-dan od [MO-yeeh pa-KE-ta] ne-DO-sta-ye.

183. I want to leave [this suitcase] here [for a few days].
Želim da ostavim [ovaj kofer] ovde [na nekoliko dana].
ZHE-leem da O-sta-veem [O-va‿ee KO-fer] OV-de [na NE-ko-lee-ko DA-na].

184. Give me a receipt for the baggage.
Dajte mi potvrdu za prtljag.
DA‿EE-te mee POT-vŭr-doo za PŬRT-l^{y}ag.

185. I have [a black trunk].
Imam [crni sanduk (OR: kovčeg)].
*EE-mam [TSŬR-nee SAN-dook (*OR: *KOV-cheg)].*

186. — four pieces of luggage altogether.
— ukupno četiri komada prtljaga.
— *OO-koop-no CHE-tee-ree ko-MA-da PŬRT-l'a-ga.*

187. Carry this to the baggage room.
Odnesite ovo u garderobu.
od-NE-see-te O-vo oo gar-de-RO-boo.

188. Don't forget that. Ne zaboravite ovo.
ne za-BO-ra-vee-te O-vo.

189. I'll carry this myself. Ovo ću poneti sam (F: sama).
O-vo t'oo PO-ne-tee sam (F: *SA-ma).*

190. Follow me. Podjite za mnom.
PO-d'ee-te za mnom.

191. Get me [a taxi]. Pozovite mi [taksi].
po-ZO-vee-te mee [TAK-see].

192. — a porter. — nosača. — *no-SA-cha.*

193. This is very fragile. Ovo je vrlo lomljivo.
O-vo ye VŬR-lo LOM-l'ee-vo.

194. Handle this carefully. Rukujte sa ovim pažljivo.
ROO-koo‿ee-te sa O-veem PAZH-l'ee-vo.

195. How much do I owe you? Koliko vam dugujem?
ko-LEE-ko vam DOO-goo-yem?

196. What is the customary tip?
Koliki je uobičajeni bakšiš (OR: napojnica)?
ko-LEE-kee ye oo-o-bee-CHA-ye-nee BAK-sheesh (OR: *NA-poy-nee-tsa)?*

TRAVEL DIRECTIONS

197. I want to go [to the Yugoslav airline office].
Želim da idem [u poslovnicu JAT-a].
ZHE-leem da EE-dem [oo PO-slov-nee-tsoo YA-ta].

198. — to the travel agency. — u putničku agenciju.
— *oo POOT-neech-koo a-GEN-tsee-yoo.*

199. — to the Yugoslav national tourist office.
— u nacionalni turistički biro (OR: Putnik).
— *oo NA-tsee-o-nal-nee too-REES-teech-kee BEE-ro (OR: POOT-neek).*

200. How long does it take to walk [to Kalemegdan]?
Koliko dugo treba da pešačim [do Kalemegdana]?
ko-LEE-ko DOO-go TRE-ba da PE-sha-cheem [do ka-le-meg-DA-na]?

201. Is this the shortest way [to Terazije Square]?
Da li je ovo najkraći put [do Terazija]?
da lee ye O-vo NA‿EE-kra-t^{y}ee poot [do te-RA-zee-ya]?

202. Show me the way [to the center of town].
Pokažite mi put [u centar grada].
po-KA-zhee-te mee poot [oo TSEN-tar GRA-da].

203. — to the shopping section (LIT.: **where the stores are).**
— gde su radnje. — *gde soo RAD-n^{y}e.*

204. Do I turn [to the north]?
Da li treba da skrenem [na sever]?
da lee TRE-ba da SKRE-nem [na SE-ver]?

205. — to the south. — na jug. — *na yoog.*

206. — to the east. — na istok. — *na EE-stok.*

207. — to the west. — na zapad. *— na ZA-pad.*

208. Which street is this? Koja je ovo ulica?
KO-ya ye O-vo OO-lee-tsa?

209. How far is it from here? Koliko je to daleko odavde?
ko-LEE-ko ye to da-LE-ko O-dav-de?

210. Is it near or far? Da li je to blizu ili daleko?
da lee ye to BLEE-zoo EE-lee da-LE-ko?

211. Can we walk there? Možemo li da pešačimo tamo?
MO-zhe-mo lee da pe-SHA-chee-mo TA-mo?

212. Am I going in the right direction (LIT.: **Am I going as I should)?**
Da li idem kako treba? *da lee EE-dem KA-ko TRE-ba?*

213. Please point. Molim vas pokažite mi.
MO-leem vas po-KA-zhee-te mee.

214. Should I go [this way] [that way]?
Da li da idem [ovim putem] [onim putem]?
da lee da EE-dem [O-veem POO-tem] [O-neem POO-tem]?

215. Turn [left] [right] at the next corner.
Skrenite [levo] [desno] na sledećem uglu.
SKRE-nee-te [LE-vo] [DE-sno] na SLE-de-t^{y}*em OO-gloo.*

216. Is it [on this side of the street]?
Da li je to [na ovoj strani ulice]?
da lee ye to [na O-voy STRA-nee OO-lee-tse]?

217. — on the other side of the street.
— na drugoj strani ulice.
— na DROO-goy STRA-nee OO-lee-tse.

218. — across the bridge. — preko mosta.
— PRE-ko MO-sta.

219. — along the boulevard. — na bulevaru.
— *na boo-le-VA-roo.*

220. — between these avenues. — izmedju ovih ulica.
— *EEZ-me-d'oo O-veeh OO-lee-tsa.*

221. — beyond the traffic light.
— posle semafora (OR: signalnog svetla).
— *PO-sle SE-ma-fo-ra (OR: seeg-NAL-nog SVE-tla).*

222. — next to the apartment house.
— do stambene zgrade. — *do STAM-be-ne ZGRA-de.*

223. — in the middle of the block.
— na sredini bloka. — *na SRE-dee-nee BLO-ka.*

224. — straight ahead. — pravo napred.
— *PRA-vo NA-pred.*

225. — inside the station. — u stanici.
— *oo STA-nee-tsee.*

226. — near the square. — blizu trga.
— *BLEE-zoo TŬR-ga.*

227. — outside the lobby. — van foajea (OR: hola).
— *van fo-a-YE-a (*OR: *HO-la).*

228. — at the entrance. — na ulazu. — *na OO-la-zoo.*

229. — opposite (LIT.: across the street from) the park.
— preko puta parka. — *PRE-ko POO-ta PAR-ka.*

230. — next to the school. — do škole. — *do SHKO-le.*

231. — in front of the monument.
— pred spomenikom. — *pred SPO-me-nee-kom.*

232. — in the rear (part) of the store.
— u zadnjem delu prodavnice (OR: radnje).
— *oo ZAD-n'em DE-loo pro-DAV-nee-tse (*OR:
RAD-n'e).

233. — behind the building.
— iza zgrade. — *EE-za ZGRA-de.*

234. — up the hill. — uzbrdo. — *OOZ-bŭr-do.*

235. — down the stairs. — niz stepenice.
— *neez STE-pe-nee-tse.*

236. — at the top of the escalator.
— na vrhu pokretnih stepenica.
— *na VŬR-hoo PO-kret-neeh STE-pe-nee-tsa.*

237. — around the traffic circle (LIT.: **traffic star).**
— oko saobraćajne zvezde.
—*O-ko SA-o-bra-t^{y}a‿ee-ne ZVE-zde.*

238. Factory. Fabrika (W: Tvornica).
FA-bree-ka (W: *TVOR-nee-tsa).*

239. Office building. Kancelarijska zgrada.
kan-tse-LA-reey-ska ZGRA-da.

240. Residential section. Stambena četvrt.
STAM-be-na CHET-vŭrt.

241. Suburbs. Predgradja (OR: Periferija).
PRED-gra-d^{y}a (OR: *pe-ree-FE-ree-ya).*

242. City. Grad. *Grad.*

243. Countryside. Selo (OR: Okolina).
SE-lo (OR: *O-ko-lee-na).*

244. Village. Selo. *SE-lo.*

BOAT

245. When must I go on board? Kad treba da se ukrcam?
kad TRE-ba da se oo-KŬR-tsam?

246. Bon voyage! Srećan put! *SRE-t'an poot!*

247. I want to rent a deck chair.
Želim da najmim šezlong.
ZHE-leem da NA‿EE-meem SHEZ-long.

248. Can we go ashore at [Split]?
Možemo li da se iskrcamo u [Splitu]?
MO-zhe-mo lee da se ees-KŬR-tsa-mo u [SPLEE-too]?

249. At what time is dinner served?
Kad se služi večera? *kad se SLOO-zhee VE-che-ra?*

250. When is [the first sitting] [the second sitting]?
Kad je [prva smena] [druga smena]?
kad ye [PŬR-va SME-na] [DROO-ga SME-na]?

251. I feel seasick. Hvata me morska bolest.
HVA-ta me MOR-ska BO-lest.

252. Do you have a remedy for seasickness?
Imate li nešto protiv morske bolesti?
EE-ma-te lee NE-shto PRO-teev MOR-ske BO-le-stee?

253. Lifeboat. Čamac za spasavanje.
CHA-mats za spa-SA-va-n'e.

254. Life preserver (LIT.: **life belt).**
Pojas za spasavanje. *PO-yas za spa-SA-va-n'e.*

255. Ferry. Trajekt. *TRA-yekt.*

256. Dock. Dok (OR: Pristanište).
*dok (*OR: *PREE-sta-nee-shte).*

257. Cabin. Kabina. *ka-BEE-na.*

258. Deck. Paluba. *PA-loo-ba.*

259. Gymnasium. Gimnastička sala (OR: Vežbaonica).
*geem-NA-steech-ka SA-la (*OR: *vezh-ba-O-nee-tsa).*

260. Pool. Bazen. *BA-zen.*

261. Captain. Kapetan. *ka-PE-tan.*

262. Purser. Blagajnik. *BLA-ga‿ee-neek.*

263. Cabin steward. Stjuart. *ST^{y}OO-art.*

264. Dining-room steward. Šef sale. *shef SA-le.*

AIRPLANE

265. I'd like [to make] [to cancel] a reservation.
Hteo (F: Htela) bih da [rezervišem] [otkažem] rezervaciju.
HTE-o (F: *HTE-la) beeh da [re-ZER-vee-shem] [OT-ka-zhem] re-zer-VA-tsee-yoo.*

266. When's the next flight to [Zagreb]?
Kad leti sledeći avion za [Zagreb]?
kad LE-tee SLE-de-t^{y}ee a-VEE-on za [ZA-greb]?

267. When does the plane arrive at [Skoplye]?
Kad stiže avion u [Skoplje]?
kad STEE-zhe a-VEE-on oo [SKO-pl^{y}e]?

268. What kind of plane is used on that flight?
Koja vrsta aviona leti na ovoj liniji?
KO-ya VŬR-sta a-vee-O-na LE-tee na O-voy LEE-nee-yee?

269. Will food be served? Da li daju hranu?
da lee DA-yoo HRA-noo?

270. May I confirm the reservation by telephone?
Mogu li da potvrdim rezervaciju telefonom?
MO-goo lee da POT-vŭr-deem re-zer-VA-tsee-yoo te-le-FO-nom?

271. At what time should we check in [at the airport]?
Kad treba da se prijavimo [na aerodromu]?
kad TRE-ba da se pree-YA-vee-mo [na A-e-ro-dro-moo[?

272. How long does it take to get to the airport from my hotel?
Koliko treba od mog hotela do aerodroma?
ko-LEE-ko TRE-ba od mog HO-te-la do A-e-ro-dro-ma?

273. Is there bus service from the airport to the city?
Ima li autobus od aerodroma u grad?
EE-ma lee a-oo-TO-boos od A-e-ro-dro-ma oo grad?

274. Is that flight [nonstop] [direct]?
Da li je taj let [nonstop] [direktan]?
da lee ye ta‿ee let [NON-stop] [dee-REK-tan]?

275. Where (LIT.: **Where all) does the plane stop en route?**
Gde sve staje avion na putu?
gde sve STA-ye a-VEE-on na POO-too?

276. How long do we stop? Koliko dugo se zadržavamo?
ko-LEE-ko DOO-go se za-dŭr-ZHA-va-mo?

277. May I stop over in [Ljubljana]?
Mogu li da prekinem let u [Ljubljani]?
MO-goo lee da PRE-kee-nem let oo [l^{y}oob-L^{y}A-nee]?

278. We want to travel [first class] [economy class].
Želimo da putujemo [prvom klasom] [drugom klasom].
ZHE-lee-mo da POO-too-ye-mo [PŬR-vom KLA-som] [DROO-gom KLA-som].

279. Is flight number [22] on time?
Da li je let broj [dvadeset dva] na vreme?
da lee ye let broy [DVA-de-set dva] na VRE-me?

280. How much baggage am I allowed?
Koliko je prtljaga dozvoljeno?
ko-LEE-ko ye PŬRT-l'a-ga DO-zvo-l'e-no?

281. How much per kilo must I pay for excess?
Koliko po kilogramu treba da platim za višak?
ko-LEE-ko po KEE-lo-gra-moo TRE-ba da PLA-teem za VEE-shak?

282. May I carry this on board?
Mogu li da ponesem ovo u avion?
MO-goo lee da po-NE-sem O-vo oo a-VEE-on?

283. Give me a seat [on the aisle].
Dajte mi sedište [kod prolaza].
DA‿EE-te mee SE-dee-shte [kod PRO-la-za].

284. — by a window. — do prozora. *— do PRO-zo-ra.*

285. — by the emergency exit.
— do izlaza u slučaju opasnosti.
— do EEZ-la-za oo SLOO-cha-yoo o-PA-sno-stee.

286. May we board the plane now (LIT.: **Are we permitted on the plane now**)**?**
Možemo li sada u avion?
MO-zhe-mo lee SA-da oo a-VEE-on?

287. From which gate does my flight leave?
Sa kojeg izlaza poleće moj avion?
sa KO-yeg EEZ-la-za PO-le-t'e moy a-VEE-on?

288. Call the stewardess. Zovite stjuardesu.
ZO-vee-te st'oo-ar-DE-soo.

289. Fasten your seat belt. Vežite pojaseve.
VE-zhee-te PO-ya-se-ve.

290. May I smoke? Smem li da pušim?
smem lee da POO-sheem?

291. Will we arrive [on time]?
Da li ćemo stići [na vreme]?
da lee T^{y}E-mo STEE-t^{y}ee [na VRE-me]?

292. — late. — kasno. — *KA-sno.*

293. Announcement. Saopštenje. *sa-op-SHTE-n^{y}e.*

294. Boarding pass. Bording karta (OR: tiket).
*BOR-deeng KAR-ta (*OR: *TEE-ket).*

295. Limousine. Limuzina. *lee-moo-ZEE-na.*

TRAIN

296. When does the ticket office [open] [close]?
Kad se [otvara] [zatvara] prodaja karata?
kad se [OT-va-ra] [ZAT-va-ra] PRO-da-ya KA-ra-ta?

297. When is the next train for [Novi Sad]?
Kad polazi sledeći voz (W: vlak) za [Novi Sad]?
*kad PO-la-zee SLE-de-t^{y}ee voz (*W: *vlak) za [NO-vee sad]?*

298. Is there [an earlier train]?
Ima li neki [raniji voz]?
EE-ma lee NE-kee [RA-nee-yee voz]?

299. — a later train. — kasniji voz.
— KA-snee-yee voz.

300. — an express train. — brzi voz. — *BŬR-zee voz.*

301. — a local train. — lokal. — *LO-kal.*

302. From which track (OR: **platform) does the train leave?**
Sa kog koloseka polazi voz?
sa kog KO-lo-se-ka PO-la-zee voz?

303. Where can I get a timetable?
Gde mogu da dobijem red vožnje?
gde MO-goo da DO-bee-yem red VO-zhn^{y}*e?*

304. Does this train stop at [Nish]?
Da li ovaj voz staje u [Nišu]?
da lee O-va‿ee voz STA-ye oo [NEE-shoo]?

305. Is there time to get off?
Imam li vremena da izadjem?
EE-mam lee VRE-me-na da ee-ZA-d^{y}*em?*

306. When do we arrive? Kad stižemo?
kad STEE-zhe-mo?

307. Is this seat (LIT.: **place) taken?**
Da li je ovo mesto zauzeto?
da lee ye O-vo ME-sto ZA-oo-ze-to?

308. Am I disturbing you? Da li vam smetam?
da lee vam SME-tam?

309. Open the window. Otvorite prozor.
ot-VO-ree-te PRO-zor.

310. Close the door. Zatvorite vrata.
zat-VO-ree-te VRA-ta.

311. Where are we now? Gde smo sada?
gde smo SA-da?

312. Is the train on time? Da li je voz na vreme?
da lee ye voz na VRE-me?

313. How late are we? Koliko kasnimo?
ko-LEE-ko KA-snee-mo?

314. Conductor. Konduktor. *kon-DOOK-tor.*

315. Gate. Peron. *PE-ron.*

316. Information office (OR: **window).**
Šalter za informacije. *SHAL-ter za een-for-MA-tsee-ye.*

317. One way ticket. Karta u jednom pravcu.
KAR-ta oo YED-nom PRAV-tsoo.

318. Round-trip ticket. Povratna karta.
PO-vrat-na KAR-ta.

319. Platform ticket. Peronska karta.
PE-ron-ska KAR-ta.

320. Railroad station.
Železnička stanica (w: Kolodvor).
ZHE-lez-neech-ka STA-nee-tsa (w: *KO-lo-dvor).*

321. Waiting room. Čekaonica. *che-ka-O-nee-tsa.*

322. Sleeping car. Spavaća kola. *SPA-va-t^{y}a KO-la.*

323. Bedroom compartment. Kušet. *KOO-shet.*

324. Smoking car. Vagon za pušenje.
VA-gon za POO-she-n^{y}e.

325. Dining car. Vagon za ručavanje.
VA-gon za roo-CHA-va-n^{y}e.

BUS, SUBWAY, STREETCAR

326. Where does [the streetcar] stop?
Gde staje [tramvaj]? *gde STA-ye [TRAM-va‿ee]?*

327. How often does [the bus] run?
Kako često ide [autobus]?
KA-ko CHE-sto EE-de [a-oo-TO-boos]?

328. [Which bus] goes to [Leskovac]?
[Koji autobus] ide u [Leskovac]?
[KO-yee a-oo-TO-boos] EE-de oo [LE-sko-vats]?

329. How much is the fare? Koliko košta karta?
ko-LEE-ko KO-shta KAR-ta?

330. Do you go near [Knez Mihailova Street]?
Da li idete blizu [Knez Mihailove ulice]?
da lee EE-de-te BLEE-zoo [knez mee-HA‿EE-lo-ve OO-lee-tse]?

331. I want to get off [at the next stop].
Želim da sidjem [na sledećoj stanici].
ZHE-leem da SEE-d^{y}*em [na SLE-de-t*^{y}*oy STA-nee-tsee].*

332. — right here. — upravo ovde.
— OO-pra-vo OV-de.

333. Please tell me where to get off.
Molim vas recite mi gde da sidjem.
MO-leem vas RE-tsee-te mee gde da SEE-d^{y}*em.*

334. Will I have to change?
Da li treba da menjam autobus?
da lee TRE-ba da ME-n^{y}*am a-oo-TO-boos?*

335. Where do we transfer? Gde presedamo?
gde pre-SE-da-mo?

336. Driver. Vozač. *VO-zach.*

337. (A) transfer. Presedanje.
pre-SE-da-n^{y}*e.*

338. Token. Žeton. *ZHE-ton.*

339. Bus stop. Autobuska stanica.
a-oo-TO-boo-ska STA-nee-tsa.

340. Where is the underpass?
Gde je podzemni prolaz?
gde ye POD-zem-nee PRO-laz?

TAXI

341. Call a taxi for me. Pozovite mi taksi.
PO-zo-vee-te mee TAK-see.

342. Are you free, driver? Da li ste slobodni, šoferu?
da lee ste SLO-bod-nee, SHO-fe-roo?

343. What do you charge [per hour]?
Koliko naplaćujete [na sat]?
ko-LEE-ko na-PLA-t^{y}oo-ye-te [na sat]?

344. — per kilometer. — na kilometar.
— na KEE-lo-me-tar.

345. — per day. — na dan. *— na dan.*

346. Take me to this address.
Odvezite me na ovu adresu.
od-VE-zee-te me na O-voo a-DRE-soo.

347. How much will the ride cost?
Koliko će koštati vožnja?
ko-LEE-ko t^{y}e KO-shta-tee VOZH-n^{y}a?

348. How long will it take us to get there?
Koliko dugo ćemo se voziti do tamo?
ko-LEE-ko DOO-go T^{y}E-mo se VO-zee-tee do TA-mo?

349. Drive us around [for one hour].
Vozite nas unaokolo [jedan sat].
VO-zee-te nas oo-NA-o-ko-lo [YE-dan sat].

350. Drive more carefully. Vozite pažljivije.
VO-zee-te pa-ZHL^{y}EE-vee-ye.

351. Drive (a little) more slowly.
Vozite malo sporije. *VO-zee-te MA-lo SPO-ree-ye.*

352. I'm [not] in a great hurry.
[Ne] žurim se. *[ne] ZHOO-reem se.*

353. Stop here. Stanite ovde. *STA-nee-te OV-de.*

354. Wait for me here. Čekajte me ovde.
CHE-ka‿ee-te me OV-de.

355. I'll return in [five minutes].
Vratiću se za [pet minuta].
VRA-tee-t^{y}oo se za [pet mee-NOO-ta].

356. Keep the change. Zadržite sitninu.
za-DŬR-zhee-te seet-NEE-noo.

357. Taxi stand. Taksi stanica. *TAK-see STA-nee-tsa.*

358. Taxi meter. Taksimetar. *TAK-see-me-tar.*

RENTING AUTOS AND OTHER VEHICLES

359. What kind of [cars] do you have?
Kakva [kola] imate?
KAK-va [KO-la] EE-ma-te?

360. I have an international driver's license.
Imam medjunarodnu vozačku dozvolu.
EE-mam me-d^{y}oo-NA-rod-noo VO-zach-koo DOZ-vo-loo.

361. What is the rate [per day]?
Koliko košta [na dan]? *ko-LEE-ko KO-shta [na dan]?*

362. How much additional [per kilometer]?
Koliki je dodatak [na kilometar]?
ko-LEE-kee ye do-DA-tak [na KEE-lo-me-tar]?

363. Are gas and oil also included?
Da li su benzin (w: petrol) i ulje uključeni?
*da lee soo BEN-zeen (*w: *PET-rol) ee OO-l^{y}e oo-KL^{Y}OO-che-nee?*

364. Does the insurance policy cover [personal liability]?
Da li osiguranje pokriva [ličnu odgovornost]?
da lee o-see-goo-RA-n^{y}e PO-kree-va [LEECH-noo od-go-VOR-nost]?

365. —property damage. —oštećenje imovine.
—o-shte-T^{y}E-n^{y}e EE-mo-vee-ne.

366. —collision. —sudar. —SOO-dar.

367. Are the papers in order?
Da li su dokumenta u redu?
da lee soo do-koo-MEN-ta oo RE-doo?

368. I'm not familiar with this car.
Ova kola mi nisu poznata.
O-va KO-la mee NEE-soo PO-zna-ta.

369. Explain [this dial]. Objasnite [ovaj brojčanik].
ob-YA-snee-te [O-va‿ee broy-CHA-neek].

370. —this mechanism. —ovaj mehanizam.
—O-va‿ee ME-ha-nee-zam.

371. Show me how [the heater] operates.
Pokažite mi kako radi [grejač].
po-KA-zhee-te mee KA-ko RA-dee [GRE-yach].

372. Will someone pick it up at the hotel?
Da li će to neko podići u hotelu?
da lee t^{y}e to NE-ko PO-dee-t^{y}ee oo HO-te-loo?

373. Is the office open all night?
Da li je biro otvoren celu noć?
da lee ye BEE-ro OT-vo-ren TSE-loo not^y?

374. Bicycle. Bicikl. *BEE-tseekl.*

375. Motorcycle. Motorcikl. *MO-tor-tseekl.*

376. Motor scooter. Vespa (OR: Velosiped).
VES-pa (OR: *ve-lo-SEE-ped).*

377. Horse and wagon. Konj i kola.
kon^y ee KO-la.

AUTO: DIRECTIONS

378. What is the name of [this city]?
Kako se zove [ovaj grad]?
KA-ko se ZO-ve [O-va‿ee grad]?

379. How far [to the next town (LIT.: **place)]?**
Koliko je daleko [sledeće mesto]?
ko-LEE-ko ye da-LE-ko [SLE-de-t^{y}e ME-sto]?

380. Where does [this road] lead?
Kuda (W: Kamo) vodi [ovaj put]?
*KOO-da (*W: *KA-mo) VO-dee [O-va‿ee poot]?*

381. Are there road signs? Da li ima putnih znakova?
da lee EE-ma POOT-neeh ZNA-ko-va?

382. Is the road [paved]? Da li je put [asfaltiran]?
da lee ye poot [as-FAL-tee-ran]?

383. — rough. — neravan. — *NE-ra-van.*

384. Show me the easiest way. Pokažite mi najlakši put.
po-KA-zhee-te mee NA‿EE-lak-shee poot.

385. Show it to me on this road map.
Pokažite mi to na putnoj karti (OR: mapi).
*po-KA-zhee-te mee to na POOT-noy KAR-tee (*OR: *MA-pee).*

386. Can I avoid heavy traffic?
Da li mogu da izbegnem veliki saobraćaj?
da lee MO-goo da EEZ-beg-nem VE-lee-kee SA-o-bra-t^{y}a‿ee?

387. May I park here [for a while]?
Da li mogu da parkiram ovde [na kratko vreme]?
da lee MO-goo da PAR-kee-ram OV-de [na KRAT-ko VRE-me]?

388. — overnight. — preko noći. — *PRE-ko NO-t^{y}ee.*

389. Approach (OR: **On ramp).**
Prilaz. *PREE-laz.*

390. Expressway. Autoput. *A-oo-to-poot.*

391. Fork. Račvanje puta. *RACH-va-n^{y}e POO-ta.*

392. Intersection. Raskrsnica (OR: Raskršće).
*RAS-kŭr-snee-tsa (*OR: *RAS-kŭr-sht^{y}e).*

393. Major road. Glavni put (W: Glavna cesta).
*GLAV-nee poot (*W: *GLAV-na TSE-sta).*

394. Garage. Garaža. *ga-RA-zha.*

395. Auto repair shop. Autoservis. *A-oo-to-SER-vees.*

396. Gas station. Benzinska stanica.
BEN-zeen-ska STA-nee-tsa.

397. Parking lot. Parkiralište. *par-KEE-ra-lee-shte.*

398. Stop sign. Stop. *stop.*

AUTO: HELP ON THE ROAD

399. My car has broken down.
Kola su mi se pokvarila (OR: Kola su mi u defektu).
*KO-la soo mee se po-KVA-ree-la (*OR: *KO-la soo mee oo de-FEK-too).*

400. Call a mechanic. Zovite mehaničara.
ZO-vee-te me-HA-nee-cha-ra.

401. Help me push the car to the side.
Pomozite mi da odguram kola u stranu.
po-MO-zee-te mee da OD-goo-ram KO-la oo STRA-noo.

402. Push me. Pogurajte me. *PO-goo-ra‿ee-te me.*

403. May I borrow [a jack]?
Da li mogu da pozajmim [dizalicu]?
da lee MO-goo da PO-za‿ee-meem [DEE-za-lee-tsoo]?

404. Change the tire. Promenite gumu.
pro-ME-nee-te GOO-moo.

405. My car is stuck [in the mud] [in a ditch].
Kola su mi se zaglavila [u blatu] [u jarku].
KO-la soo mee se za-GLA-vee-la [oo BLA-too] [oo YAR-koo].

406. Drive me to the nearest gas station.
Odvezite me do najbliže benzinske stanice.
od-VE-zee-te me do NA‿EE-blee-zhe BEN-zeen-ske STA-nee-tse.

AUTO: GAS STATION AND REPAIR SHOP

407. Give me twenty liters of [regular] [premium] gasoline.
Dajte mi dvadeset litara [standardnog] [premium] benzina.
DA‿EE-te mee DVA-de-set LEE-ta-ra [STAN-dard-nog] [PRE-mee-oom] BEN-zee-na.

408. —diesel fuel. —dizel benzina.
—DEE-zel BEN-zee-na.

409. Fill it up. Napunite. *na-POO-nee-te.*

410. Check the oil. Proverite ulje.
PRO-ve-ree-te OO-l'e.

411. Lubricate the car. Podmažite kola.
POD-ma-zhee-te KO-la.

412. Put water in the radiator. Stavite vodu u radijator.
STA-vee-te VO-doo oo ra-dee-YA-tor.

413. Recharge the battery. Napunite akumulator.
na-POO-nee-te a-koo-MOO-la-tor.

414. Clean the windshield.
Očistite šoferšajbnu (OR: vetrobran).
*o-CHEE-stee-te SHO-fer-sha‿eeb-noo (*OR: *VE-tro-bran).*

415. Adjust the brakes. Podesite kočnice.
PO-de-see-te KOCH-nee-tse.

416. Check the tire pressure.
Proverite pritisak u gumama.
PRO-ve-ree-te PREE-tee-sak oo GOO-ma-ma.

417. Repair the flat tire. Zakrpite defektnu gumu.
ZA-kŭr-pee-te de-FEKT-noo GOO-moo.

418. Could you wash [the car] [the windshield] now?
Da li možete sada da operete [kola] [vetrobran]?
da lee MO-zhe-te SA-da da O-pe-re-te [KO-la] [VE-tro-bran]?

419. How long must we wait?
Koliko dugo moramo da čekamo?
ko-LEE-ko DOO-go MO-ra-mo da-CHE-ka-mo?

420. The motor overheats. Motor se pregrejava. *MO-tor se pre-GRE-ya-va.*

421. Is there a leak? Da li curi? *da lee TSOO-ree?*

422. It makes noise. Suviše je bučno. *SOO-vee-she ye BOOCH-no.*

423. The lights don't work. Svetla ne rade. *SVET-la ne RA-de.*

424. The car doesn't start. Auto neće da se upali. *A-oo-to NE-t*^{y}*e da se oo-PA-lee.*

AUTO: PARTS OF THE CAR (AND AUTO EQUIPMENT)

425. Accelerator. Akselerator (OR: Gasna pedala). *ak-SE-le-ra-tor (*OR: *GA-sna pe-DA-la).*

426. Air filter. Filter za vazduh. *FEEL-ter za VAZ-dooh.*

427. Alcohol. Alkohol. *AL-ko-hol.*

428. Antifreeze. Antifriz. *AN-tee-freez.*

429. Axle. Osovina. *o-SO-vee-na.*

430. Battery. Akumulator. *a-koo-MOO-la-tor.*

431. Bolt. Gvozden klin. *GVOZ-den kleen.*

432. [Emergency] brake. [Rezervna] kočnica. *[RE-zer-vna] KOCH-nee-tsa.*

433. Foot —. Nožna —. *NOZH-na —.*

434. Hand —. Ručna —. *ROOCH-na —.*

435. Bumper. Branik. *BRA-neek.*

436. Carburator. Karburator. *kar-BOO-ra-tor.*

437. Chasis. Šasija. *SHA-see-ya.*

438. Choke (automatic). Čok (OR:Saug). *chok (*OR: *SA-oog).*

439. Clutch. Kuplung. *KOOP-loong.*

440. Cylinder. Cilindar. *tsee-LEEN-dar.*

441. Differential. Diferencijal. *dee-fe-ren-TSEE-yal.*

442. Directional signal. Migavac. *MEE-ga-vats.*

443. Door. Vrata. *VRA-ta.*

444. Electrical system. Električni sistem. *e-LEK-treech-nee SEE-stem.*

445. Engine (OR: **Motor).** Motor. *MO-tor.*

446. Exhaust pipe. Auspuh (OR: Izduvna cev). *A-oo-spooh (*OR: *EEZ-doov-na tsev).*

447. Exterior. Spoljašnost. *SPO-l'a-shnost.*

448. Fan. Ventilator. *ven-TEE-la-tor.*

449. Fan belt. Remen ventilatora. *RE-men ven-TEE-la-to-ra.*

450. Fender. Branik. *BRA-neek.*

451. Flashlight. Džepna (OR: Signalna) lampa. *DZHEP-na (*OR: *SEEG-nal-na) LAM-pa.*

452. Fuel pump. Benzinska pumpa. *BEN-zeen-ska POOM-pa.*

453. Fuse. Osigurač. *o-see-GOO-rach.*

454. Gas tank. Rezervoar. *re-zer-VO-ar.*

455. Gear shift. Menjač brzine. *ME-n^{y}ach bŭr-ZEE-ne.*

456. [First] gear. [Prva] brzina. *[PŬR-va] bŭr-ZEE-na.*

457. Second —. Druga —. *DROO-ga —.*

458. Third —. Treća —. *TRE-t^{y}a —.*

459. Fourth —. Četvrta —. *CHET-vŭr-ta —.*

460. Reverse gear. Rikverc. *REEK-verts.*

461. Neutral gear. Neutral. *NE-oo-tral.*

462. Grease. Mazivo. *MA-zee-vo.*

463. Generator. Generator. *ge-NE-ra-tor.*

464. Hammer. Čekić. *CHE-keet^y.*

465. Heater. Grejač. *GRE-yach.*

466. Hood. Hauba. *HA-oo-ba.*

467. Horn. Truba. *TROO-ba.*

468. Horsepower. Konjska snaga. *KON^y-ska SNA-ga.*

469. Ignition key. Ključ za paljenje.
kl^{y}ooch za PA-l^{y}e-n^{y}e.

470. Inner tube. Unutrašnja guma.
OO-noo-tra-shn^{y}a GOO-ma.

471. Instrument panel. Tabla za instrumente.
TA-bla za een-stroo-MEN-te.

472. License plate. Registarska tabla.
RE-gee-star-ska TA-bla.

473. Light. Svetlo. *SVET-lo.*

474. Headlight. Far. *far.*

475. Parking light. Svetlo za parkiranje.
SVET-lo za par-KEE-ra-n^{y}e.

476. Brake light. Stop svetlo. *stop SVET-lo.*

477. Taillight. Zadnje svetlo. *ZAD-n^{y}e SVET-lo.*

478. Rear-view mirror. Retrovizor. *re-tro-VEE-zor.*

479. Side-view mirror.
Bočno ogledalo (OR: Bočni retrovizor).
BOCH-no o-GLE-da-lo (OR: *BOCH-nee re-tro-VEE-zor).*

480. Muffler. Prigušivač. *pree-goo-SHEE-vach.*

481. Nail. Ekser (W: Čavao). *EK-ser* (W: *CHA-va-o).*

482. Nut. Matica. *MA-tee-tsa.*

483. Pedal. Pedala. *pe-DA-la.*

484. Pliers. Kliješta. *KL^{y}E-shta.*

485. Radiator. Hladnjak (OR: Kiler).
HLAD-n^{y}ak (OR: *KEE-ler).*

486. Radio. Radio. *RA-dee-o.*

487. Rags. Krpe. *KŬR-pe.*

488. Rope. Konopac. *KO-no-pats.*

489. Screw. Šraf. *shraf.*

490. Screwdriver. Šrafciger. *SHRAF-tsee-ger.*

491. Shock absorber. Amortizer. *a-mor-TEE-zer.*

492. Skid chains. Kočni lanac za sneg.
KOCH-nee LA-nats za sneg.

493. Snow tires. Gume za sneg. *GOO-me za sneg.*

494. Spark plugs. Svećice. *SVE-t^{y}ee-tse.*

495. Speedometer. Brzinomer. *BŬR-zee-no-mer.*

496. Starter. Starter. *STAR-ter.*

497. Steering wheel. Volan. *VO-lan.*

498. Tire. Guma. *GOO-ma.*

499. [Spare] [Tubeless] tire. [Rezervna] [Puna] guma. *[RE-zer-vna] [POO-na] GOO-ma.*

500. Tire pump. Pumpa za gume. *POOM-pa za GOO-me.*

501. Tools. Alat. *A-lat.*

502. Automatic transmission. Automatski prenos (OR: menjač). *a-oo-TO-mat-skee PRE-nos (*OR: *ME-n^{y}ach).*

503. Standard (OR: **manual) transmission.** Ručni prenos (OR: menjač). *ROOCH-nee PRE-nos (*OR: *ME-n^{y}ach).*

504. Trunk. Kofer (OR: Gepek). *KO-fer* (OR: *GE-pek).*

505. Valve. Ventil. *VEN-teel.*

506. Water-cooling system. Sistem za hladjenje. *SEE-stem za HLA-d^{y}e-n^{y}e.*

507. [Front] [Rear] wheel. [Prednji] [Zadnji] točak. *[PRED-n^{y}ee] [ZAD-n^{y}ee] TO-chak.*

508. Windshield wiper. Brisač. *BREE-sach.*

509. Wrench. Francuski ključ. *FRAN-tsoo-skee kl^{y}ooch.*

MAIL

510. Where is [the post office] [a mail box]? Gde je [pošta] [poštansko sanduče]? *gde ye [PO-shta] [PO-shtan-sko SAN-doo-che]?*

511. To which window should I go?
Na koji šalter da idem?
na KO-yee SHAL-ter da EE-dem?

512. I want to send this letter [by surface mail].
Želim da pošaljem ovo pismo [običnom poštom].
ZHE-leem da PO-sha-lʸem O-vo PEE-smo [O-beech-nom PO-shtom].

513. — by air mail. — avionom. — *a-vee-O-nom.*

514. — by special delivery.
— hitnom (OR: ekspres) pošiljkom.
— *HEET-nom* (OR: *EK-spres) PO-sheelʸ-kom.*

515. — by registered mail. — preporučeno.
— *pre-PO-roo-che-no.*

516. — by parcel post. — paketnom poštom.
— *PA-ket-nom PO-shtom.*

517. How much postage do I need [for this postcard]?
Kolika je poštarina [za ovu dopisnicu]?
ko-LEE-ka ye PO-shta-ree-na [za O-voo DO-pee-snee-tsoo]?

518. The package contains [printed matter] [fragile material].
Paket sadrži [štampane stvari] [lomljive stvari].
PA-ket SA-dŭr-zhee [SHTAM-pa-ne STVA-ree] [LOM-lʸee-ve STVA-ree].

519. I want to insure this for [1000 dinars].
Želim da osiguram ovo na [hiljadu dinara].
ZHE-leem da o-see-GOO-ram O-vo na [HEE-lʸa-doo DEE-na-ra].

520. Will it go out [today]? Da li će otići [danas]?
da lee tʸe O-tee-tʸee [DA-nas]?

521. Give me ten [100-dinar] stamps.
Dajte mi deset poštanskih maraka [od sto dinara].
DA‿EE-te mee DE-set PO-shtan-skeeh MA-ra-ka [od sto DEE-na-ra].

522. Where can I get a money order?
Gde mogu da dobijem novčanu uputnicu?
gde MO-goo da DO-bee-yem NOV-cha-noo OO-poot-nee-tsoo?

523. Please forward my mail to [Los Angeles].
Molim vas pošaljite moju poštu u [Los Andjeles].
MO-leem vas PO-sha-l^{y}ee-te MO-yoo PO-shtoo oo [los AN-d^{y}e-les].

524. The American Express office will hold my mail.
Biro Amerikan Ekspresa će sačuvati moju poštu.
BEE-ro a-ME-ree-kan ek-SPRE-sa t^{y}e SA-choo-va-tee MO-yoo PO-shtoo.

TELEGRAM

525. I'd like to send [a telegram].
Želim da pošaljem [telegram (w: brzojav)].
ZHE-leem da PO-sha-l^{y}em [TE-le-gram (w: *BŬR-zo-yav)].*

526. —a night letter. —prekonoćno pismo.
—pre-ko-NOT^y-no PEE-smo.

527. —a cablegram. —telegram pismo.
— TE-le-gram PEE-smo.

528. What is the rate per word? Koliko košta jedna reč?
ko-LEE-ko KO-shta YED-na rech?

529. What is the minimum charge?
Koja je minimalna tarifa?
KO-ya ye MEE-nee-mal-na ta-REE-fa?

530. When will an ordinary telegram reach [London]?
Kad će običan telegram stići u [London]?
kad t^{y}e O-bee-chan TE-le-gram STEE-t^{y}ee oo [LON-don]?

TELEPHONE

531. May I use the telephone?
Mogu li da se poslužim telefonom?
MO-goo lee da se PO-sloo-zheem te-le-FO-nom?

532. Will you dial this number for me?
Hoćete li mi nazvati ovaj broj?
HO-t^{y}e-te lee mee NA-zva-tee O-va‿ee broy?

533. Operator (LIT.: **Miss), get me this number.**
Gospodjice, nazovite mi ovaj broj.
GO-spo-d^{y}ee-tse, na-ZO-vee-te mee O-va‿ee broy.

534. Call me at this number.
Nazovite me na ovaj broj.
na-ZO-vee-te me na O-va‿ee broy.

535. My telephone number is [123-456].
Broj mog telefona je [jedan dva tri - četiri pet šest].
broy mog te-le-FO-na ye [YE-dan dva tree - CHE-tee-ree pet shest].

536. How much is a (long-distance) call to [Chicago]?
Koliko košta razgovor sa [Čikagom]?
ko-LEE-ko KO-shta RAZ-go-vor sa [chee-KA-gom]?

537. What is the charge for the first three minutes?
Koliko košta prva tri minuta?
ko-LEE-ko KO-shta PŬR-va tree mee-NOO-ta?

538. I want to reverse the charges (OR: **make a collect call).**
Želim da govorim na račun druge strane.
ZHE-leem da GO-vo-reem na RA-choon DROO-ge STRA-ne.

539. Bill me at my home phone number.
Stavite ovo na račun mog kućnog broja telefona.
STA-vee-te O-vo na RA-choon mog KOO-t^{y}nog BRO-ya te-le-FO-na.

540. They don't answer. Niko ne odgovara.
NEE-ko ne od-GO-va-ra.

541. The line is busy. Linija je zauzeta.
LEE-nee-ya ye ZA-oo-ze-ta.

542. Hello (on the telephone). Halo. *HA-lo.*

543. You've given me the wrong number.
Dali ste mi pogrešan broj.
DA-lee ste mee PO-gre-shan broy.

544. This is [Jovan] speaking. Ovde [Jovan].
OV-de [YO-van].

545. With whom do you want to speak?
S kim želite da govorite?
s keem ZHE-lee-te da GO-vo-ree-te?

546. Hold the line (LIT.: **Wait).** Pričekajte.
PRE-che-ka‿ee-te.

547. Dial again. Nazovite opet. *na-ZO-vee-te O-pet.*

548. I can't hear you. Ne mogu da vas čujem.
ne MO-goo da vas CHOO-yem.

549. The connection is poor. Veza je slaba.
VE-za ye SLA-ba.

550. Speak louder. Govorite glasnije.
GO-vo-ree-te GLA-snee-ye.

551. Call [him] [her] to the phone.
Zovite [ga] [je] na telefon.
ZO-vee-te [ga] [ye] na te-LE-fon.

552. He's not here. On nije ovde. *on NEE-ye OV-de.*

553. There's a telephone call for you.
Telefonski poziv za vas. *te-LE-fon-skee PO-zeev za vas.*

554. May I leave a message?
Mogu li da ostavim poruku?
MO-goo lee da O-sta-veem PO-roo-koo?

555. Call me back as soon as possible.
Nazovite me opet što pre.
na-ZO-vee-te me O-pet shto pre.

556. I'll call back later. Zvaću vas opet kasnije.
ZVA-t'oo vas O-pet KA-snee-ye.

557. I'll wait for your call until [six] o'clock.
Čekaću na vaš poziv do [šest] sati.
CHE-ka-t'oo na vash PO-zeev do [shest] SA-tee.

HOTEL

558. I'm looking for [a good hotel].
Tražim [dobar hotel].
TRA-zheem [DO-bar HO-tel].

559. — the best hotel. — najbolji hotel.
— *NA‿EE-bo-l^{y}ee HO-tel.*

560. — an inexpensive hotel. — jevtin hotel.
— *YEV-teen HO-tel.*

561. — a boarding house (OR: **pension).**
— pansion. *PAN-see-on.*

562. I want to be in the center of town.
Želim da budem u centru grada.
ZHE-leem da BOO-dem oo TSEN-troo GRA-da.

563. I want a quiet location. Želim tiho mesto.
ZHE-leem TEE-ho ME-sto.

564. I prefer to be close to [the university].
Volim da budem blizu [univerziteta].
VO-leem da BOO-dem BLEE-zoo [oo-nee-ver-zee-TE-ta].

565. I have a reservation for tonight.
Imam rezervaciju za noćas.
EE-mam re-zer-VA-tsee-yoo za NO-t^{y}as.

566. Where is the registration desk?
Gde je recepcija? *gde ye re-TSEP-tsee-ya?*

567. Fill out this registration form.
Ispunite ovaj formular.
ee-SPOO-nee-te O-va‿ee for-MOO-lar.

568. Sign here. Potpišite ovde.
pot-PEE-shee-te OV-de.

569. Leave your passport. Ostavite svoj pasoš ovde.
O-sta-vee-te svoy PA-sosh OV-de.

570. You may pick it up later.
Možete ga podići kasnije.
MO-zhe-te ga PO-dee-t^{y}ee KA-snee-ye.

571. Do you have [a single room]?
Da li imate [jednokrevetnu sobu]?
da lee EE-ma-te [yed-no-KRE-vet-noo SO-boo]?

572. — a double room. — dvokrevetnu sobu.
— DVO-kre-vet-noo SO-boo.

573. — an air-conditioned room.
— sobu sa klima uredjajem.
— SO-boo sa KLEE-ma OO-re-d^{y}a-yem.

574. — a suite. — apartman. *— a-PART-man.*

575. — a quiet room. — tihu sobu.
— TEE-hoo SO-boo.

576. — an inside room (LIT.: **a room not looking onto the street).**
— sobu koja ne gleda na ulicu.
— SO-boo KO-ya ne GLE-da na OO-lee-tsoo.

577. — an outside room (LIT: **a room looking onto the street).**
— sobu koja gleda na ulicu.
— SO-boo KO-ya GLE-da na OO-lee-tsoo.

578. — a room with a pretty view.
— sobu s lepim pogledom.
— SO-boo s LE-peem PO-gle-dom.

579. I want a room [with a double bed].
Želim sobu [s duplim krevetom].
ZHE-leem SO-boo [s DOO-pleem KRE-ve-tom].

580. — with twin beds. — sa dva kreveta.
— sa dva KRE-ve-ta.

581. — with a bath. — sa kupatilom (W: kupaonom).
— sa KOO-pa-tee-lom (W: *KOO-pa-o-nom).*

582. — with a shower. — sa tušem. *— sa TOO-shem.*

583. — with running water. — sa tekućom vodom.
— sa TE-koo-t^{y}om VO-dom.

584. — with hot water. — sa toplom vodom.
— sa TO-plom VO-dom.

585. — with a balcony. — sa balkonom.
— sa bal-KO-nom.

586. — with television. — sa televizorom.
— sa te-le-VEE-zo-rom.

587. I'll take a room [for one night].
Uzeću sobu [za jednu noć].
OO-ze-t^{y}oo SO-boo [za YED-noo not^y].

588. — for several days. — na nekoliko dana.
— na NE-ko-lee-ko DA-na.

589. — for a week or so. — otprilike na nedelju.
— ot-PREE-lee-ke na NE-de-l^{y}oo.

590. Can I have it [with meals]?
Da li mogu da imam sobu [sa hranom]?
da lee MO-goo da EE-mam SO-boo [sa HRA-nom]?

591. — without meals. — bez hrane. *— bez HRA-ne.*

592. — with breakfast only. — samo sa doručkom.
— SA-mo sa DO-rooch-kom.

593. What is the rate [per night]?
Koliko košta [za noć]? *ko-LEE-ko KO-shta [za not^y]?*

594. — per week. — za nedelju. *— za NE-de-l^{y}oo.*

595. — per month. — za mesec. *— za ME-sets.*

596. Are tax and service included?
Da li su taksa i servis uključeni?
da lee soo TAK-sa ee SER-vees oo-KL^{y}OO-che-nee?

597. I'd like to see the room.
Želim da vidim sobu. *ZHE-leem da VEE-deem SO-boo.*

598. Do you have something [better]?
Da li imate nešto [bolje]?
da lee EE-ma-te NE-shto [BO-l^y*e]?*

599. — cheaper. — jevtinije. *— yev-TEE-nee-ye.*

600. — larger. — veće. *— VE-*t^y*e.*

601. — smaller. — manje. *— MA-*n^y*e.*

602. — on a [lower] [higher] floor.
— na [nižem] [višem] spratu.
— na [NEE-zhem] [VEE-shem] SPRA-too.

603. — with more light. — sa više svetla.
— sa VEE-she SVET-la.

604. — with more air. — sa više vazduha.
— sa VEE-she VAZ-doo-ha.

605. — more attractively furnished.
— sa lepšim nameštajem.
— sa LEP-sheem NA-me-shta-yem.

606. — with a view of the sea.
— s pogledom na more. *s PO-gle-dom na MO-re.*

607. It's too noisy. Suviše je bučno.
SOO-vee-she ye BOOCH-no.

608. This is satisfactory. Ovo je zadovoljavajuće.
O-vo ye za-do-vo-L^y*A-va-yoo-*t^y*e.*

609. Is there [an elevator]? Ima li [lift]?
EE-ma lee [leeft]?

610. Upstairs. Na spratu. *na SPRA-too.*

611. Downstairs. Dole. *DO-le.*

612. What is my room number?
Koji je broj moje sobe?
KO-yee ye broy MO-ye SO-be?

613. Give me my room key.
Dajte mi ključ moje sobe.
DA‿EE-te mee klʸooch MO-ye SO-be.

614. Bring my luggage to my room.
Ponesite moj prtljag u moju sobu.
PO-ne-see-te moy PŬRT-lʸag oo MO-yoo SO-boo.

615. Tell the chambermaid to get my room ready.
Recite sobarici da spremi moju sobu.
RE-tsee-te SO-ba-ree-tsee da SPRE-mee MO-yoo SO-boo.

616. Wake me [at eight in the morning].
Probudite me [u osam ujutro].
pro-BOO-dee-te me [oo O-sam OO-yoo-tro].

617. Don't disturb me until then.
Ne uznemiravajte me dotle.
ne oo-zne-MEE-ra-va‿ee-te me DOT-le.

618. I want [breakfast] in my room.
Želim [doručak] u mojoj sobi.
ZHE-leem [DO-roo-chak] oo MO-yoy SO-bee.

619. Room service, please. Servis, molim vas.
SER-vees, MO-leem vas.

620. Bring me [some ice cubes].
Donesite mi [leda]. *do-NE-see-te mee [LE-da].*

621. I want to speak to [the manager] [your superior].
Želim da govorim sa [direktorom] [vašim pretpostavljenim].
ZHE-leem da GO-vo-reem sa [DEE-rek-to-rom] [VA-sheem pret-PO-stav-lʸe-neem].

622. Do you have [a letter] for me?
Imate li [pismo] za mene?
EE-ma-te lee [PEE-smo] za ME-ne?

623. — a message. — poruku. — *PO-roo-koo.*

624. — a package. — paket. — *PA-ket.*

625. Send [a chambermaid]. Pošaljite [sobaricu].
PO-sha-l'ee-te [SO-ba-ree-tsoo].

626. — a valet. — sobara. — *SO-ba-ra.*

627. — a bellhop. — dečka. — *DECH-ka.*

628. — a waiter. — kelnera (w: konobara).
— *KEL-ne-ra* (w: *KO-no-ba-ra).*

629. — a porter. — nosača. — *no-SA-cha.*

630. — a messenger. — kurira. — *KOO-ree-ra.*

631. I am expecting [a friend]. Očekujem [prijatelja].
o-CHE-koo-yem [PREE-ya-te-l'a].

632. — a guest. — gosta. — *GO-sta.*

633. — a telephone call. — telefonski poziv.
— *te-LE-fon-skee PO-zeev.*

634. Has anyone called (telephoned)?
Da li me neko zvao? *da lee me NE-ko ZVA-o?*

635. Send [him] [her] up. Pošaljite [ga] [je] gore.
PO-sha-l'ee-te [ga] [ye] GO-re.

636. I won't be here for lunch. Neću biti ovde za ručak.
NE-t'oo BEE-tee OV-de za ROO-chak.

637. May I leave [these valuables] in the hotel safe?
Da li mogu da ostavim [ove stvari od vrednosti] u hotelskom sefu?
da lee MO-goo da O-sta-veem [O-ve STVA-ree od VRED-no-stee] oo HO-tel-skom SE-foo?

638. I'd like to get [my possessions] from the safe.
Želim da uzmem [svoje stvari] iz sefa.
ZHE-leem da OO-zmem [SVO-ye STVA-ree] eez SE-fa.

639. When must I check out? Kad treba da se odjavim?
kad TRE-ba da se OD-ya-veem?

640. I'm leaving [at 10 o'clock]. Odlazim [u deset sati].
OD-la-zeem [oo DE-set SA-tee].

641. Make out my bill [as soon as possible].
Spremite moj račun [što pre].
SPRE-mee-te moy RA-choon [shto pre].

642. Cashier. Blagajnik. *BLA-ga‿ee-neek.*

643. Doorman. Vratar. *VRA-tar.*

CHAMBERMAID

644. The door doesn't lock.
Vrata ne mogu da se zaključaju.
VRA-ta ne MO-goo da se za-KL^{y}OO-cha-yoo.

645. The [toilet] doesn't work.
[Toalet (OR: WC)] ne radi.
[to-A-let (OR: *VE-tse)] ne RA-dee.*

646. The room is [too cold] [too hot].
Soba je suviše [hladna] [topla].
SO-ba ye SOO-vee-she [HLAD-na] [TO-pla].

647. Is this drinking water? Da li je ovo voda za piće?
da lee ye O-vo VO-da za PEE-t^{y}e?

648. There is no hot water. Nema vruće vode.
NE-ma VROO-t^{y}e VO-de.

649. Spray [for insects] [for vermin].
Poprskajte protiv [insekata] [gamadi].
po-PŬR-ska‿ee-te PRO-teev (EEN-se-ka-ta] [GA-ma-dee].

650. Wash and iron [this shirt].
Operite i ispeglajte [ovu košulju].
o-PE-ree-te ee ee-SPE-gla‿ee-te [O-voo KO-shoo-lʸoo].

651. Change the sheets. Promenite čaršave.
pro-ME-nee-te CHAR-sha-ve.

652. Make the bed. Raspremite krevet.
ras-PRE-mee-te KRE-vet.

653. Bring me [another blanket].
Donesite mi [još jedno ćebe (w: još jednu deku)].
DO-ne-see-te mee [yosh YED-no Tʸ E-be (w: *yosh YED-noo DE-koo)].*

654. — a bath mat. — prostirku za kupatilo.
— PRO-steer-koo za KOO-pa-tee-lo.

655. — a bed sheet. — krevetski čaršav.
— KRE-vet-skee CHAR-shav.

656. — a candle. — sveću. *— SVE-tʸoo.*

657. — some coat hangers. — nekoliko vešalica.
— NE-ko-lee-ko VE-sha-lee-tsa.

658. — glass. — čašu. *— CHA-shoo.*

659. — a pillow. — jastuk. *— YA-stook.*

660. — a pillowcase. — jastučnicu.
— YA-stooch-nee-tsoo.

661. — an adaptor for electrical appliances.
— transformator. *— trans-FOR-ma-tor.*

662. — some soap. — nešto sapuna.
— *NE-shto sa-POO-na.*

663. — some toilet paper. — nešto toalet papira.
— *NE-shto to-A-let pa-PEE-ra.*

664. — towel. — peškir (W: Ubrus).
— *PE-shkeer* (W: *OO-broos).*

665. — washcloth. — peškirić. — *pe-SHKEE-reet^y^.*

RENTING AN APARTMENT

666. I want to rent [a furnished] [an unfurnished] apartment [with a bathroom].
Želim da iznajmim stan [sa nameštajem] [bez nameštaja] [sa kupatilom].
ZHE-leem da eez-NA‿EE-meem stan [sa NA-me-shta-yem] [bez NA-me-shta-ya] [sa KOO-pa-tee-lom].

667. — with two bedrooms.
— sa dve spavaće sobe (OR: dvosobni).
— *sa dve SPA-va-t^y^e SO-be* (OR: *DVO-sob-nee).*

668. — with a living room.
— sa salonom (OR: sa dnevnom sobom).
— *sa sa-LO-nom* (OR: *sa DNEV-nom SO-bom).*

669. — with a dining room.
— sa trpezarijom (OR: salom za ručavanje).
— *sa tŭr-pe-ZA-ree-yom* (OR: *SA-lom za roo-CHA-va-n^y^e).*

670. — with a kitchen. — sa kujnom (W: kuhinjom).
— sa KOO‿EE-nom (W: *KOO-hee-n^{y}om).*

671. Do you furnish [the linen]?
Da li je vaša [posteljina]?
da lee ye VA-sha [PO-ste-l^{y}ee-na]?

672. — the dishes (OR: **china).**
— posudje (OR: kujnski pribor).
— PO-soo-d^{y}e (OR: *KOO‿EEN-skee PREE-bor).*

673. Do we have to sign a lease (LIT.: **a contract)?**
Da li moramo da potpišemo ugovor?
da lee MO-ra-mo da POT-pee-she-mo OO-go-vor?

APARTMENT: USEFUL WORDS

674. Alarm clock. Budilnik. *BOO-deel-neek.*

675. Ashtray. Pepeljara. *pe-PE-l^{y}a-ra.*

676. Bathtub. Kada. *KA-da.*

677. Bottle opener. Otvarač za flaše.
ot-VA-rach za FLA-she.

678. Broom. Metla. *MET-la.*

679. Can opener. Otvarač za konzerve.
ot-VA-rach za KON-zer-ve.

680. Chair. Stolica. *STO-lee-tsa.*

681. Chest of drawers. Orman (W: Ormar).
OR-man (W: *OR-mar).*

682. Clock. Sat (OR: Časovnik).
sat (OR: *cha-SOV-neek).*

683. Closet. Plakar (OR: Orman [W: Ormar] u zidu).
PLA-kar (OR: *OR-man* [W: *OR-mar] oo ZEE-doo).*

684. Cook.
Kuvar (F: Kuvarica) (W: Kuhar; F: Kuharica).
KOO-var (F: *KOO-va-ree-tsa)* (W: *KOO-har;* F: *KOO-ha-ree-tsa).*

685. Cork (stopper). Zapušač (OR: Čep).
za-POO-shach (OR: *chep).*

686. Corkscrew. Vadičep. *VA-dee-chep.*

687. Curtains. Zavese. *ZA-ve-se.*

688. Cushion. Jastuk. *YA-stook.*

689. Dishwasher. Mašina za pranje sudova.
ma-SHEE-na za PRA-n^{y}e SOO-do-va.

690. Doorbell. Zvonce na vratima.
ZVON-tse na VRA-tee-ma.

691. Drapes. Draperija. *dra-PE-ree-ya.*

692. Dryer. Mašina za sušenje.
ma-SHEE-na za SOO-she-n^{y}e.

693. Fan. Ventilator. *ven-TEE-la-tor.*

694. Floor. Pod. *pod.*

695. Hassock. Jastuče za sedenje.
YA-stoo-che za SE-de-n^{y}e.

696. Lamp. Lampa. *LAM-pa.*

697. Light bulb. Sijalica (W: Žarulja).
SEE-ya-lee-tsa (W: *ZHA-roo-l^{y}a).*

698. Linens (OR: **bedding).** Posteljina (W: Plahte).
po-STE-l^{y}ee-na (W: *PLAH-te).*

699. Mosquito net. Mreža za komarce.
MRE-zha za ko-MAR-tse.

700. Pail. Kofa. *KO-fa.*

701. Rug. Tepih (OR: Ćilim, Tapison).
TE-peeh (OR: *T'EE-leem, ta-pee-SON).*

702. Sink. Sudoper (OR: Slivnik na česmi).
soo-DO-per (OR: *SLEEV-neek na CHE-smee).*

703. Switch (light). Prekidač (OR: Šalter).
pre-KEE-dach (OR: *SHAL-ter).*

704. Table. Sto. *sto.*

705. Tablecloth. Stolnjak (OR: Stoni čaršav).
STOL-n'ak (OR: *STO-nee CHAR-shav).*

706. Terrace. Balkon (OR: Terasa).
BAL-kon (OR: *te-RA-sa).*

707. Tray. Poslužavnik. *po-SLOO-zhav-neek.*

708. Vase. Vaza. *VA-za.*

709. Venetian blinds (OR: **Window shades).**
Roletne (OR: Žaluzine) (W: Rebrenice).
ro-LET-ne (OR: *zha-loo-ZEE-ne)* (W: *re-BRE-nee-tse).*

710. Washing machine. Mašina za pranje veša.
ma-SHEE-na za PRA-n'e VE-sha.

711. Whisk broom. Četkica. *CHET-kee-tsa.*

CAFÉ AND BAR

712. Bartender, I'd like [something to drink].
Barman, želim [nešto da popijem].
BAR-man, ZHE-leem [NE-shto da PO-pee-yem].

713. — a cocktail. — koktel. — *KOK-tel.*

714. — a bottle of mineral water [without gas]. — flašu kisele (OR: bocu mineralne) vode [negazirane]. — *FLA-shoo KEE-se-le* (OR: *BO-tsoo MEE-ne-ral-ne) VO-de [ne-ga-ZEE-ra-ne].*

715. — a whiskey [and soda]. — viski [sa sodom]. — *VEE-skee [sa SO-dom].*

716. — a cognac. — konjak. — *KO-n^{y}ak.*

717. — a brandy. — rakiju. — *RA-kee-yoo.*

718. — a grape brandy. — lozovaču. — *LO-zo-va-choo.*

719. — a juniper brandy. — klekovaču. — *KLE-ko-va-choo.*

720. — a plum brandy. — šljivovicu. — *SHL^{y}EE-vo-vee-tsoo.*

721. — a wine brandy. — vinjak. — *VEE-n^{y}ak.*

722. — a liqueur. — liker. — *LEE-ker.*

723. — a gin and tonic. — džin i tonik. — *dzheen ee TO-neek.*

724. — rum. — rum. — *room.*

725. — Scotch whiskey. — škotski viski. — *SHKOT-skee VEE-skee.*

726. — rye whiskey. — raženi viski. — *RA-zhe-nee VEE-skee.*

727. — Bourbon whiskey. — burbon viski. — *BOOR-bon VEE-skee.*

728. — vodka. — votku. — *VOT-koo.*

729. — a lemonade. — limunadu. — *lee-moo-NA-doo.*

730. — a nonalcoholic drink. — bezalkoholno piće. — *bez-AL-ko-hol-no PEE-t^{y}e.*

731. — a bottled fruit drink. — flašu voćnog soka. — *FLA-shoo VOT^y-nog SO-ka.*

732. — a [light] [draft] beer. — [svetlo] [točeno] pivo. — *[SVET-lo] [TO-che-no] PEE-vo.*

733. — a dark beer. — crno pivo. — *TSŬR-no PEE-vo.*

734. — champagne. — šampanjac. — *sham-PA-n^{y}ats.*

735. — a glass of sherry. — čašu šerija. — *CHA-shoo SHE-ree-ya.*

736. — [red] [white] [rosé] wine.
— [crno] [belo] [ružica] vino.
— *[TSŬR-no] [BE-lo] [ROO-zhee-tsa] VEE-no.*

737. Let's have another. Da popijemo još jedno piće.
da PO-pee-ye-mo yosh YED-no PEE-t^{y}e.

738. To your health! (OR: **Cheers!**)
Živeli! (OR: U vaše zdravlje!)
ZHEE-ve-lee! (OR: *oo VA-she ZDRAV-l^{y}e!)*

RESTAURANT

739. Can you recommend a good [Serbian] restaurant [for dinner]?
Da li možete da mi preporučite dobar [srpski] restoran [za večeru]?
da lee MO-zhe-te da mee pre-PO-roo-chee-te DO-bar [SŬRP-skee] re-STO-ran [za VE-che-roo]?

740. — for breakfast. — za doručak.
— za DO-roo-chak.

741. — for a snack (OR: **a sandwich).**
— za užinu (OR: sendvič).
— za OO-zhee-noo (OR: *SEND-veech).*

742. Do you serve [lunch]? Da li služite [ručak]?
da lee SLOO-zhee-te [ROO-chak]?

743. What time is [supper] served?
Kad se služi [večera]? *kad se SLOO-zhee [VE-che-ra]?*

744. There are [three] of us. Ima nas [troje].
EE-ma nas [TRO-ye].

745. Are you [my waiter] [my waitress]?
Jeste li vi [moj kelner (W: konobar)] [moja kelnerica (W: konobarica)]?
YE-ste lee vee [moy KEL-ner (W: *KO-no-bar)] [MO-ya KEL-ne-ree-tsa* (W: *KO-no-ba-ree-tsa)]?*

746. I prefer a table [by the window].
Volim sto [pored prozora].
VO-leem sto [PO-red PRO-zo-ra].

747. — in the corner. — u uglu. *— oo OO-gloo.*

748. — outdoors. — napolju. *— NA-po-l'oo.*

749. — indoors. — unutra. *— oo-NOO-tra.*

750. I'd like to wash my hands.
Želim da operem ruke. *ZHE-leem da O-pe-rem ROO-ke.*

751. We want to dine à la carte.
Želimo da večeramo à la carte (OR: po meniu).
ZHE-lee-mo da VE-che-ra-mo "à la carte" (OR: *po ME-nee-oo).*

752. We want to eat lightly. Želimo lako da jedemo.
Zhe-lee-mo LA-ko da YE-de-mo.

753. What is the specialty of the house?
Koji je specijalitet ovog restorana?
KO-yee ye spe-tsee-ya-LEE-tet O-vog re-sto-RA-na?

754. What kind of [fish] do you have?
Koju vrstu [ribe] imate?
KO-yoo VŬR-stoo [REE-be] EE-ma-te?

755. Serve us as quickly as you can.
Poslužite nas što pre.
PO-sloo-zhee-te nas shto pre.

756. Call the wine steward. Zovite kelnera za vino.
ZO-vee-te KEL-ne-ra za VEE-no.

757. Bring me [the menu] [the wine list].
Donesite mi [meni] [vinsku listu].
do-NE-see-te mee [ME-nee] [VEEN-skoo LEE-stoo].

758. — water [with ice] [without ice].
— vodu [sa ledom] [bez leda].
— *VO-doo [sa LE-dom] [bez LE-da].*

759. — a napkin. — salvetu. — *sal-VE-too.*

760. — bread. — hleba. — *HLE-ba.*

761. — butter. — putera (w: maslaca).
— *POO-te-ra* (w: *MA-sla-tsa).*

762. — a cup. — šolju. — *SHO-*l^y*oo.*

763. — a fork. — viljušku (w: vilicu).
— *VEE-*l^y*oo-shkoo* (w: *VEE-lee-tsoo).*

764. — a glass. — čašu. — *CHA-shoo.*

765. — a [sharp] knife. — [oštar] nož.
— *[O-shtar] nozh.*

766. — a plate. — tanjir. — *TA-n^{y}eer.*

767. — a saucer. — tacnu. — *TATS-noo.*

768. — a spoon. — kašiku (w: žlicu).
KA-shee-koo (w: *ZHLEE-tsoo).*

769. — a soup spoon (OR: **tablespoon).**
— veliku kašiku (za supu).
— *VE-lee-koo KA-shee-koo (za SOO-poo).*

770. — a teaspoon. — kašičicu za čaj.
— *KA-shee-chee-tsoo za cha‿ee.*

771. I want something [plain].
Želim nešto [jednostavno].
ZHE-leem NE-shto [YED-no-stav-no].

772. — without meat. — bez mesa. — *bez ME-sa.*

773. Is it [canned]? Da li je [iz konzerve]?
da lee ye [eez KON-zer-ve]?

774. — fatty (OR: **greasy).** — masno. — *MA-sno.*

775. — fresh. — sveže. — *SVE-zhe.*

776. — frozen. — smrznuto. — *SMŬR-znoo-to.*

777. — lean. — posno (OR: mršavo).
PO-sno (OR: *MŬR-sha-vo).*

778. — peppery. — ljuto. — *L^{y}OO-to.*

779. — [very] salty. — [vrlo] slano.
— *[VŬR-lo] SLA-no.*

780. — spicy. — začinjeno. — *za-CHEE-n^{y}e-no.*

781. — [very] sweet. — [vrlo] slatko.
— *[VŬR-lo] SLAT-ko.*

782. How is it prepared? Kako je spremljeno?
KA-ko ye SPREM-l^{y}e-no?

783. Is it [baked]? Da li je [pečeno]?
da lee ye [PE-che-no]?

784. —boiled. —kuvano. —*KOO-va-no.*

785. —breaded. —pohovano. —*PO-ho-va-no.*

786. —chopped. —iseckano. —*EE-sets-ka-no.*

787. —fried. —prženo. —*PŬR-zhe-no.*

788. —grilled. —na roštilju. —*na ro-SHTEE-l^{y}oo.*

789. —ground. —mleveno. —*MLE-ve-no.*

790. —roasted. —pečeno. —*PE-che-no.*

791. —sautéed. —sotirano. *so-TEE-ra-no.*

792. —on a skewer. —na ražnju. —*na RAZH-n^{y}oo.*

793. This is [stale]. Ovo je [bajato]. *O-vo ye [BA-ya-to].*

794. —too tough. —suviše žilavo.
—*SOO-vee-she ZHEE-la-vo.*

795. —too dry. —suviše suvo.
—*SOO-vee-she SOO-vo.*

796. I like the meet [rare]. Želim meso [nedopečeno].
ZHE-leem ME-so [ne-do-PE-che-no].

797. —medium. —srednje. —*SRED-n^{y}e.*

798. —well done. —dobro pečeno.
—*DO-bro PE-che-no.*

799. This is [undercooked] [burned].
Ovo je [nedokuvano] [izgorelo].
O-vo ye [ne-do-KOO-va-no] [eez-GO-re-lo].

800. A little more. Još malo. *yosh MA-lo.*

801. A little less. Malo manje. *MA-lo MA-n^{y}e.*

802. Something else. Nešto drugo. *NE-shto DROO-go.*

803. A small portion. Malu porciju.
MA-loo POR-tsee-yoo.

804. The next course. Sledeće jelo. *SLE-de-t'ye YE-lo.*

805. I've had enough.
Dosta sam jeo (F: jela) (OR:Sit [F: Sita] sam).
DO-sta sam YE-o (F: *YE-la)* (OR: *seet* [F: *SEE-ta] sam).*

806. This is [not clean] [dirty]. Ovo je [nečisto] [prljavo].
O-vo ye [NE-chee-sto] [PŬR-l'ya-vo].

807. This is cold. Ovo je hladno. *O-vo ye HLAD-no.*

808. I didn't order this. Nisam ovo poručio (F: poručila).
NEE-sam O-vo po-ROO-chee-o (F: *po-ROO-chee-la).*

809. You may take this away. Možete da odnesete.
MO-zhe-te da od-NE-se-te.

810. May I exchange this for [a salad]?
Mogu li da zamenim ovo [za salatu]?
MO-goo lee da ZA-me-neem O-vo [za sa-LA-too]?

811. What flavors [of ice cream] do you have?
Koje vrste [sladoleda] imate?
KO-ye VŬR-ste [SLA-do-le-da] EE-ma-te?

812. The check, please. Račun, molim vas.
RA-choon, MO-leem vas.

813. Pay at the cashier's desk. Platite na blagajni.
PLA-tee-te na BLA-ga‿ee-nee.

814. Is the tip included? Da li je servis uključen?
da lee ye SER-vees OO-kl'yoo-chen?

815. There's a mistake in the bill.
Ima jedna greška u računu.
EE-ma YED-na GRE-shka oo ra-CHOO-noo.

816. What are these charges for?
Zašto ste mi ovo naplatili?
ZA-shto ste mee O-vo na-PLA-tee-lee?

817. The food and service were excellent.
Hrana i servis su bili odlični.
HRA-na ee SER-vees soo BEE-lee OD-leech-nee.

818. Hearty appetite! Prijatno! *PREE-yat-no!*

FOOD: SEASONINGS

819. Condiments. Začini. *ZA-chee-nee.*

820. Catsup. Kečap. *KE-chap.*

821. Garlic. Beli luk (w: Češnjak).
BE-lee look (w: *CHESH-n^y^ak).*

822. Mayonnaise. Majonez. *ma-YO-nez.*

823. [Hot] [mild] mustard. [Ljuti] [blagi] senf.
[L^y^OO-tee] [BLA-gee] senf.

824. Oil. Ulje (OR: Zejtin). *OO-l^y^e* (OR: *ZEY-teen).*

825. Pepper. Biber. *BEE-ber.*

826. Salt. So. *so.*

827. Sauce. Sos. *sos.*

828. Sugar. Šećer. *SHE-t^y^er.*

829. Vinegar. Sirće (w: Ocat). *SEER-t^y^e* (w: *O-tsat).*

BEVERAGES AND BREAKFAST FOODS

The following sections are alphabetized according to the main words in the Serbo-Croatian entries to aid you in reading menus.

830. Čaj [sa kremom]. *cha‿ee [sa KRE-mom].* Tea [with cream].

831. — sa limunom. *— sa LEE-moo-nom.* — with lemon.

832. — sa mlekom. *— sa MLE-kom.* — with milk.

833. — sa saharinom. *— sa sa-ha-REE-nom.* — with an artificial sweetener.

834. Hladan čaj. *— HLA-dan cha‿ee.* Iced tea.

835. Džem. *dzhem.* Jam.

836. Gibanica. *GEE-ba-nee-tsa.* Cheese pie.

837. Grepfrut sok. *GREP-froot sok.* Grapefruit juice.

838. [Crni] [beli] hleb. *[TSŬR-nee] [BE-lee] hleb.* [Dark] [White] bread.

839. [Kuvana] jaja. *KOO-va-na YA-ya.* [Poached] eggs.

840. Pržena —. *PŬR-zhe-na —.* Fried —.

841. Rovita —. *RO-vee-ta —.* Soft-boiled —.

842. Tvrda —. *TVŬR-da —.* Hard-boiled —.

843. [Crna] kafa (w: Kava). *[TSŬR-na] KA-fa* (w: *KA-va).* [Black] coffee.

844. Hladan ajs-kafe. *HLA-dan A‿EES-ka-fe.* Iced coffee.

845. Kajgana. *KA‿EE-ga-na.* Scrambled eggs.

846. Kajmak. *KA‿EE-mak.* Local cream cheese.

847. Kajzerice. *KA‿EE-ze-ree-tse.* Rolls.

848. Kolači. *ko-LA-chee.* Pastry.

849. Kruh (W). *krooh.* Bread.

850. Marmelada. *mar-me-LA-da.* Marmalade.

851. Omlet. *OM-let.* Omelet.

852. Palačinke. *pa-la-CHEEN-ke.* Pancakes (OR: Crêpes).

853. Pekmez. *PEK-mez.* Jam.

854. Prepržen hleb. *PRE-pŭr-zhen hleb.* Toast.

855. Proja. *PRO-ya.* Corn bread.

856. Slanina [sa jajima]. *SLA-nee-na [sa YA-yee-ma].* Bacon [and eggs].

857. Sok od narandže. *sok od NA-ran-dzhe.* Orange juice.

858. Sok od paradajza. *sok od pa-ra-DA‿EE-za.* Tomato juice.

859. Sok od rajčice (W). *sok od RA‿EE-chee-tse.* Tomato juice.

860. Srpski sir. *SŬRP-skee seer.* Feta cheese.

861. Šunka. *SHOON-ka.* Ham.

862. Tost. *tost.* Toast.

863. Voćni sok. *VOT^{y}-nee sok.* Fruit juice.

864. Vruća čokolada. *VROO-t^{y}a cho-ko-LA-da.* Hot chocolate.

865. [Meke] [tvrde] zemičke. *[ME-ke] [TVŬR-de] ZE-meech-ke.* [Soft] [Hard] rolls.

866. [Kuvane] [Suve] žitne pahuljice. *[KOO-va-ne] [SOO-ve] ZHEET-ne PA-hoo-l^{y}ee-tse.* [Cooked] [Dry] cereal.

SOUPS AND SALADS

867. Čorba od povrća. *CHOR-ba od PO-vŭr-t^{y}a.* Vegetable soup.

868. Konzomé. *kon-zo-ME.* Consomé.

869. Krompir salata. *KROM-peer sa-LA-ta.* Potato salad.

870. Paradajz čorba. *pa-ra-DA‿EEZ CHOR-ba.* Tomato soup.

871. Paradajz salata. *pa-ra-DA‿EEZ sa-LA-ta.* Tomato salad.

872. Pileća čorba. *PEE-le-t^{y}a CHOR-ba.* Chicken soup.

873. Preliv za salatu. *PRE-leev za sa-LA-too.* Salad dressing.

874. Salata od morske ribe. *sa-LA-ta od MOR-ske REE-be.* Seafood salad.

875. Salata od piletine. *sa-LA-ta od PEE-le-tee-ne.* Chicken salad.

876. Salata od račića. *sa-LA-ta od RA-chee-t^{y}a.* Shrimp salad.

877. [Govedja] supa. *[GO-ve-d^{y}a] SOO-pa.* [Beef] broth.

878. Višisoaz. *vee-shee-so-AZ.* Vichyssoise.

879. Zelena salata. *ZE-le-na sa-LA-ta.* Green salad.

MEATS AND MEAT DISHES

880. Beli bubrezi. *BE-lee BOO-bre-zee.* Pork testicles.

881. Biftek. *BEEF-tek.* Steak.

882. Bubrezi. *BOO-bre-zee.* Kidneys.

883. Ćevapčići. *t^{y}e-VAP-chee-t^{y}ee.* Grilled meat rolls.

884. Ćufte. *T^{y}OOF-te.* Meatballs.

885. Ćulbastija. *t^{y}ool-BA-stee-ya.* Grilled veal or pork.

886. Dalmatinski pršut. *dal-MA-teen-skee PŬR-shoot.* Dalmatian smoked ham.

887. Divljač. *DEEV-l^{y}ach.* Game (OR: Venison).

888. Djuveč. *D^{y}OO-vech.* Stew with rice and vegetables.

889. Džigerica. *DZHEE-ge-ree-tsa.* Liver.

890. Faširane šnicle. *FA-shee-ra-ne SHNEE-tsle.* Fried meat patties.

891. Govedina. *GO-ve-dee-na.* Beef.

892. Govedje pečenje. *go-VE-d^{y}e pe-CHE-nye.* Roast beef.

893. Jagnjetina. *YAG-n^{y}e-tee-na.* Lamb.

894. Jetra. *YE-tra.* Liver.

895. Kobasice. *ko-BA-see-tse.* Sausage.

896. Kotleti. *ko-TLE-tee.* Cutlets (OR: Chops).

897. Krmenadle. *kŭr-me-NA-dle.* Chops.

898. Leskovačka mućkalica. *LE-sko-vech-ka MOOT^{y}-ka-lee-tsa.* Hot shredded pork Leskovac style.

899. Meso od divljači. *ME-so od DEEV-l^{y}a-chee.* Venison.

900. Mlevena govedina. *MLE-ve-na GO-ve-dee-na.* Ground beef.

901. Mozak. *MO-zak.* Brains.

902. Musaka [od krompira]. *moo-SA-ka [od krom-PEE-ra].* [Potato] moussaka.

903. — od plavih patlidžana. *— od PLA-veeh pat-lee-DZHA-na.* Eggplant —.

904. Ovčetina. *OV-che-tee-na.* Mutton.

905. Pljeskavica. *PLYE-ska-vee-tsa.* Grilled meat patty, often spicy.

906. Pohovani mozak. *PO-ho-va-nee MO-zak.* Breaded brains.

907. Praseće pečenje. *PRA-se-t^{y}e pe-CHE-nye.* Roast suckling pig.

908. Pršuta. *PŬR-shoo-ta.* Smoked ham.

909. Punjene [paprike]. *POO-n^{y}e-ne [PA-pree-ke].* [Peppers] stuffed with minced meat.

910. — tikvice. — *TEEK-vee-tse.* Zucchini —.

911. Ražnjići. *razh-N^{y}EE-t^{y}ee.* Shish kebab (without vegetables).

912. Sarma. *SAR-ma.* Stuffed cabbage.

913. Srce. *SŬR-tse.* Heart.

914. Svinjetina. *SVEE-n^{y}e-tee-na.* Pork.

915. Škembići. *shkem-BEE-t^{y}ee.* Tripe.

916. Štruca od mesa. *SHTROO-tsa od ME-sa.* Meat loaf.

917. Šunka. *SHOON-ka.* Ham.

918. Teletina. *TE-le-tee-na.* Veal.

919. Vešalica. *VE-sha-lee-tsa.* Grilled smoked veal or pork.

POULTRY

920. Ćuretina. *T^{y}OO-re-tee-na.* Turkey.

921. Golub. *GO-loob.* Pigeon.

922. Guska. *GOO-ska.* Goose.

923. Patka. *PAT-ka.* Duck.

924. Piletina. *PEE-le-tee-na.* Chicken.

FISH AND SEAFOOD

925. **Bakalar.** *ba-KA-lar.* Cod.

926. **Brancin.** *BRAN-tseen.* Bass.

927. **Dagnje.** *DAG-n^{y}e.* Mussels.

928. **Haringa.** *HA-reen-ga.* Herring.

929. **Iverka.** *EE-ver-ka.* Halibut.

930. **Jastog.** *YA-stog.* Lobster.

931. **List.** *leest.* Sole.

932. **Losos.** *LO-sos.* Salmon.

933. **Lubin.** *LOO-been.* Bass.

934. **Mušule.** *MOO-shoo-le.* Mussels.

935. **Ostrige.** *O-stree-ge.* Oysters.

936. **Pastrmka.** *PA-stŭrm-ka.* Trout.

937. **Puževi.** *POO-zhe-vee.* Snails.

938. **Račići.** *RA-chee-t^{y}ee.* Shrimp.

939. **Rak.** *rak.* Crab.

940. **Rečni rak.** *RECH-nee rak.* Crayfish.

941. **Sabljarka.** *sab-L^{y}AR-ka.* Swordfish.

942. **Sardine.** *sar-DEE-ne.* Sardine.

943. **Skampi.** *SKAM-pee.* Shrimp.

944. **Svoja.** *SVO-ya.* Halibut.

945. **Školjke.** *SHKOL^y-ke.* Clams.

946. **Tunjevina.** *TOO-n^{y}e-vee-na.* Tuna.

VEGETABLES AND STARCHES

947. **Artičoke.** *ar-tee-CHO-ke.* Artichokes.

948. **Bamja.** *BAM-ya.* Okra.

949. **Boranija.** *bo-RA-nee-ya.* Green (OR: Lima) beans.

950. **Celer.** *TSE-ler.* Celery.

951. **Crni luk.** *TSŬR-nee look.* Onions.

952. **Gljive.** *GL'EE-ve.* Mushrooms.

953. **Grah** (W). *grah.* Beans.

954. **Grašak.** *GRA-shak.* Peas.

955. **Karfiol.** *kar-FEE-ol.* Cauliflower.

956. **Knedle.** *KNED-le.* Dumplings.

957. **Krastavci.** *KRA-stav-tsee.* Cucumbers.

958. **Krompir** (W: **Krumpir).**
KROM-peer (W: *KROOM-peer).* Potatoes.

959. **[Kuvan] krompir.** *[KOO-van] KROM-peer.* [Boiled] potatoes.

960. **Pečen —.** *PE-chen —.* Baked —.

961. **Pržen —.** *PŬR-zhen —.* Fried —.

962. **Punjen —.** *POO-n'en —.* Stuffed —.

963. **Pire od krompira.** *PEE-re od krom-PEE-ra.* Mashed potatoes.

964. **Kupus.** *KOO-poos.* Cabbage.

965. **Masline.** *MA-slee-ne.* Olives.

966. **Mrkve.** *MŬRK-ve.* Carrots.

967. **Paprike.** *PA-pree-ke.* Green peppers.

968. Paradajz. *pa-ra-DA‿EEZ.* Tomatoes.

969. Pasulj. *PA-sool*^{y}. Beans.

970. Pečurke. *PE-choor-ke.* Mushrooms.

971. Peršun (W: **Peršin**). *PER-shoon* (W: *PER-sheen).* Parsley.

972. Pirinač. *PEE-ree-nach.* Rice.

973. Rajčica. *RA‿EE-chee-tsa.* Tomatoes.

974. Rezanci. *re-ZAN-tsee.* Noodles.

975. Riža (W). *REE-zha.* Rice.

976. Špageti. *shpa-GE-tee.* Spaghetti.

977. Spanać. *SPA-nat*^{y}. Spinach.

978. Šargarepe. *shar-ga-RE-pe.* Carrots.

979. Špargle. *SHPAR-gle.* Asparagus.

980. Špinat (W). *SHPEE-nat.* Spinach.

981. Zelena salata. *ZE-le-na sa-LA-ta.* Lettuce.

982. Zeleni grah (W). *ZE-le-nee grah.* Green (OR: Lima) beans.

983. Žuta boranija. *ZHOO-ta bo-RA-nee-ya.* Wax (OR: Yellow) beans.

FRUITS

984. Ananas. *A-na-nas.* Pineapple.

985. Banana. *ba-NA-na.* Banana.

986. Breskva. *BRE-skva.* Peach.

987. Dinja. *DEE-n^{y}a.* Cantaloupe.

988. [Pola] grepfruta. *[PO-la] GREP-froo-^{t}a.* [A half] grapefruit.

989. Grožđje. *GROZH-d^{y}e.* Grapes.

990. Jabuka. *YA-boo-ka.* Apple.

991. Jagode. *YA-go-de.* Strawberries.

992. Kajsija. *KA‿EE-see-ya.* Apricot.

993. Kruška. *KROO-shka.* Pear.

994. Limun. *LEE-moon.* Lemon.

995. Lubenica. *loo-BE-nee-tsa.* Watermelon.

996. Maline. *MA-lee-ne.* Raspberries.

997. Mandarine. *man-da-REE-ne.* Tangerine.

998. Mango. *MAN-go.* Mango.

999. Marelica. *MA-re-lee-tsa.* Apricot.

1000. Narandža. *na-RAN-dzha.* Orange.

1001. Papaja. *pa-PA-ya.* Papaya.

1002. Pomorandža. *po-mo-RAN-dzha.* Orange.

1003. Smokve. *SMOK-ve.* Figs.

1004. Suve šljive. *SOO-ve SHL^{y}EE-ve.* Prunes.

1005. Šljive. *SHL^{y}EE-ve.* Plums.

1006. Trešnje. *TRE-shn^{y}e.* Cherries.

1007. Urme. *OOR-me.* Dates.

DESSERTS

1008. Biskviti. *bee-SKVEE-tee.* Cookies.

1009. Keksi. *KEK-see.* Cookies.

1010. Kolač. *KO-lach.* Cake.

1011. Kolači. *ko-LA-chee.* French pastry.

1012. Krem od vanile. *krem od va-NEE-le.* Custard.

1013. Palačinke. *pa-la-CHEEN-ke.* Crêpes (OR: Pancakes).

1014. [Francusko] pecivo. *[FRAN-tsoo-sko] PE-tsee-vo.* [French] pastry.

1015. Pita [sa jabukama]. *PEE-ta [sa YA-boo-ka-ma].* [Apple] pie.

1016. —sa orasima. *—sa O-ra-see-ma.* Walnut —.

1017. Puding. *POO-deeng.* Pudding.

1018. [Mlad] [Zreo] sir. *[mlad] [ZRE-o] seer.* [Mild] [Sharp] cheese.

1019. Sladoled [od vanilije] [od čokolade]. *SLA-do-led [od va-NEE-lee-ye] [od cho-ko-LA-de].* [Vanilla] [Chocolate] ice cream.

1020. Šerbet. *SHER-bet.* Sherbet.

1021. Torta. *TOR-ta.* Cake.

SIGHTSEEING

1022. I want a licensed guide [who speaks English].
Želim registrovanog vodiča [koji govori engleski].
ZHE-leem RE-gee-stro-va-nog vo-DEE-cha [KO-yee GO-vo-ree ENG-le-skee].

1023. How long will the excursion take?
Koliko će trajati izlet?
ko-LEE-ko t'e TRA-ya-tee EEZ-let?

1024. Do I need to book in advance?
Da li moram da rezervišem unapred?
da lee MO-ram da re-ZER-vee-shem OO-na-pred?

1025. Are admission tickets [and a snack] included?
Da li su ulaznice [i zakuska] uključeni?
da lee soo OO-laz-nee-tse [ee ZA-koo-ska] oo-KL'OO-che-nee?

1026. What is the charge for a trip [to the island]?
Koliko košta put [na ostrvo]?
ko-LEE-ko KO-shta poot [na O-stŭr-vo]?

1027. —to the mountain. —u planine.
—oo PLA-nee-ne.

1028. —to the sea. —na more. *—na MO-re.*

1029. —around the city. —po gradu. *—po GRA-doo.*

1030. Call for me [tomorrow] at my hotel at 8 A.M.
Nazovite me [sutra] u mom hotelu u osam ujutro.
na-ZO-vee-te me [SOO-tra] oo mom HO-te-loo oo O-sam OO-yoo-tro.

1031. Show me the sights of interest [in the town].
Pokažite mi znamenitosti [grada].
PO-ka-zhee-te mee ZNA-me-nee-to-stee [GRA-da].

1032. What is that building? Šta je ta zgrada?
shta ye ta ZGRA-da?

1033. How old is it? Koliko je stara?
ko-LEE-ko ye STA-ra?

1034. Can we go in? Možemo li da udjemo?
MO-zhe-mo lee da OO-d^{y}e-mo?

1035. I'm interested in [architecture].
Interesuje me [arhitektura].
EEn-te-re-soo-ye me [ar-hee-tek-TOO-ra].

1036. — archeology. — arheologija.
— ar-he-o-LO-gee-ya.

1037. — sculpture. — vajarstvo. *— va-YAR-stvo.*

1038. — painting. — slikarstvo. *— slee-KAR-stvo.*

1039. — folk art. — narodna umetnost.
— NA-rod-na OO-met-nost.

1040. — arts and crafts. — domaća radinost.
— DO-ma-t^{y}a RA-dee-nost.

1041. — modern art. — moderna umetnost.
— MO-der-na OO-met-nost.

1042. I'd like to see [the park]. Želim da vidim [park].
ZHE-leem da VEE-deem [park].

1043. — the cathedral. — katedralu. *— ka-te-DRA-loo.*

1044. — the countryside. — okolinu. *— o-ko-LEE-noo.*

1045. — the library. — biblioteku.
— bee-blee-o-TE-koo.

1046. — the ruins. — ruševine. *— roo-SHE-vee-ne.*

1047. — the castle. — zamak. *— ZA-mak.*

1048. — the palace.
— palatu (W: palaču) (OR: dvorac).
— *PA-la-too* (W: *PA-la-choo)* (OR: *DVO-rats).*

1049. — the zoo. — zoološki vrt. — *zo-o-LO-shkee vŭrt.*

1050. Let's take a walk around [the botanical garden].
Hajde da se prošetamo [po botaničkoj bašti].
HA‿EE-de da se PRO-she-ta-mo [po bo-TA-neech-koy BA-shtee].

1051. Is it a tourist trap? Da li je to klopka za turiste?
da lee ye to KLOP-ka za TOO-ree-ste?

1052. A beautiful view! Divan pogled!
DEE-van PO-gled!

1053. Very interesting! Vrlo interesantno!
VŬR-lo een-te-re-SANT-no!

1054. Magnificent! Sjajno! *S^{y}A‿EE-no!*

1055. We're enjoying ourselves. Mi se lepo provodimo.
mee se LE-po pro-VO-dee-mo.

1056. I'm bored. Dosadno mi je. *DO-sad-no mee ye.*

1057. When does the museum [open] [close]?
Kad se muzej [otvara] [zatvara]?
kad se MOO-zey [OT-va-ra] [ZAT-va-ra]?

1058. Is this the way to [the entrance] [the exit]?
Da li je ovo put ka [ulazu] [izlazu]?
da lee ye O-vo poot ka [OO-la-zoo] [EEZ-la-zoo]?

1059. Let's visit the fine arts gallery.
Hajde da posetimo galeriju likovne umetnosti.
HA‿EE-de da PO-se-tee-mo GA-le-ree-yoo LEE-kov-ne OO-met-no-stee.

1060. Let's stay longer. Ostanimo duže.
O-sta-nee-mo DOO-zhe.

1061. Let's leave now. Hajde da idemo.
HA‿EE-de da EE-de-mo.

1062. We must be back by [5 o'clock].
Moramo da se vratimo do [pet sati].
MO-ra-mo da se VRA-tee-mo do [pet SA-tee].

1063. If there is time, let's rest a while.
Hajde da se odmorimo malo ako imamo vremena.
HA‿EE-de da se OD-mo-ree-mo MA-lo A-ko EE-ma-mo VRE-me-na.

WORSHIP

1064. Altar. Oltar. *OL-tar.*

1065. Catholic church. Katolička crkva.
KA-to-leech-ka TSŬR-kva.

1066. Choral music. Horska muzika.
HOR-ska MOO-zee-ka.

1067. Collection plate. Tas za priloge.
tas za PREE-lo-ge.

1068. Communion. Pričešće (OR: Pričest).
PREE-che-sht'e (OR: *PREE-chest).*

1069. Confession. Ispoved (OR: Ispovest).
EE-spo-ved (OR: *EE-spo-vest).*

1070. Contribution. Prilog. *PREE-log.*

1071. Mass (Catholic). Misa. *MEE-sa.*

1072. Minister. Protestanski sveštenik.
pro-te-STANT-skee SVE-shte-neek.

1073. Prayers. Molitve. *MO-leet-ve.*

1074. Prayer book. Molitvenik. *MO-leet-ve-neek.*

1075. Priest. Sveštenik (W: Svećenik).
SVE-shte-neek (W: *SVE-t^{y}e-neek).*

1076. Protestant church. Protestantska crkva.
pro-te-STANT-ska TSŬR-kva.

1077. Rabbi. Rabin. *RA-been.*

1078. Religious school. Verska škola.
VER-ska SHKO-la.

1079. Sermon. Propoved. *PRO-po-ved.*

1080. Services (Orthodox). Služba. *SLOOZḤ-ba.*

1081. Sunday (OR: **Church) school.**
Nedeljna (OR: Crkvena) škola.
NE-del^y-na (OR: *TSŬR-kve-na) SHKO-la.*

1082. Synagogue. Sinagoga. *see-na-GO-ga.*

ENTERTAINMENT

1083. Is there [a matinée] today?
Da li danas ima [matine]?
da lee DA-nas EE-ma [ma-TEE-ne]?

1084. Has [the show] begun?
Da li je [predstava] počela?
da lee ye [PRED-sta-va] PO-che-la?

1085. What's playing today?
Šta se danas daje (OR: prikazuje)?
shta se DA-nas DA-ye (OR: *pree-KA-zoo-ye)?*

1086. Do you have any seats for this evening?
Imate li sedišta (OR: mesta) za večeras?
EE-ma-te lee SE-dee-shta (OR: *ME-sta) za ve-CHE-ras?*

1087. How much is [an orchestra seat]?
Koliko košta sedište [u parteru]?
ko-LEE-ko KO-shta SE-dee-shte [oo par-TE-roo]?

1088. — a balcony seat. — na balkonu.
— na bal-KO-noo.

1089. — a box. — u loži. *— oo LO-zhee.*

1090. — a seat in the mezzanine. — u mezaninu.
— oo me-za-NEE-noo.

1091. Not too far from the stage.
Ne suviše daleko od pozornice.
ne SOO-vee-she da-LE-ko od PO-zor-nee-tse.

1092. Here is my ticket. Evo moje karte.
E-vo MO-ye KAR-te.

1093. Can I see and hear well from there?
Da li mogu dobro da vidim i da čujem odatle?
da lee MO-goo DO-bro da VEE-deem ee da CHOO-yem O-dat-le?

1094. Follow [the usher]. Idite za [razvodnikom].
EE-dee-te za [RAZ-vod-nee-kom].

1095. Is smoking permitted here?
Da li je ovde dozvoljeno pušenje?
da lee ye OV-de DO-zvo-l^y*e-no POO-she-*n^y*e?*

1096. How long is the intermission?
Koliko traje pauza? *ko-LEE-ko TRA-ye PA-oo-za?*

1097. When does the program [begin] [end]?
Kad [počinje] [se svršava] program?
kad [PO-chee-n^y*e] [se SVŬR-sha-va] PRO-gram?*

1098. Everyone enjoyed the show.
Svima se dopala predstava.
SVEE-ma se DO-pa-la PRED-sta-va.

1099. Ballet. Balet. *BA-let.*

1100. Box office. Blagajna (OR: Kasa).
BLA-ga‿ee-na (OR: *KA-sa).*

1101. Circus. Cirkus. *TSEER-koos.*

1102. Concert. Koncert. *KON-tsert.*

1103. Gambling casino. Kockarnica.
KOTS-kar-nee-tsa.

1104. The [beginning] [end] of the line.
[Početak] [Kraj] reda. *[po-CHE-tak] [kra‿ee] RE-da.*

1105. Movies. Bioskop (W: Kino).
BEE-o-skop (W: *KEE-no).*

1106. Musical comedy. Opereta. *o-pe-RE-ta.*

1107. Nightclub. Bar. *bar.*

1108. Opera. Opera. *O-pe-ra.*

1109. Opera glasses. Dvogled (W: Dalekozor) za operu.
DVO-gled (W: *DA-le-ko-zor) za O-pe-roo.*

1110. Opera house. Zgrada opere. *ZGRA-da O-pe-re.*

1111. Performance. Predstava. *PRED-sta-va.*

1112. Program. Program. *PRO-gram.*

1113. Puppet show. Predstava u pozorištu lutaka.
PRED-sta-va oo PO-zo-ree-shtoo LOO-ta-ka.

1114. Reserved seat. Rezervisano sedište (OR: mesto).
re-ZER-vee-sa-no SE-dee-shte (OR: *ME-sto).*

1115. Sports event. Sportska priredba.
SPORT-ska PREE-red-ba.

1116. Standing room. Stajanje. *STA-ya-n^{y}e.*

1117. Theater. Pozorište (w: Kazalište). *PO-zo-ree-shte* (w: *KA-za-lee-shte).*

1118. Ticket window. Šalter za ulaznice. *SHAL-ter za OO-la-znee-tse.*

1119. Variety show. Variete. *va-ree-e-TE.*

NIGHTCLUB AND DANCING

1120. How much is [the admission charge]?
Koliko košta [ulaznica]?
ko-LEE-ko KO-shta [OO-laz-nee-tsa]?

1121. — the cover (OR: **minimum) charge.**
— konzumacija. *— kon-zoo-MA-tsee-ya.*

1122. Is there a floor show? Ima li programa?
EE-ma lee PRO-gra-ma?

1123. Where can we go to dance?
Kuda (w: Kamo) možemo da idemo da igramo (w: plešemo)?
KOO-da (w: *KA-mo) MO-zhe-mo da EE-de-mo da EE-gra-mo* (w: *PLE-she-mo)?*

1124. May I have this dance?
Mogu li da igram ovu igru sa vama?
MO-goo lee da EE-gram O-voo EE-groo sa VA-ma?

1125. You dance very well. Vi igrate vrlo dobro.
vee EE-gra-te VŬR-lo DO-bro.

1126. Will you play [a fox-trot]?
Hoćete li da svirate [fokstrot]?
HO-t^{y}e-te lee da SVEE-ra-te [FOK-strot]?

1127. — a rumba. — rumbu. — *ROOM-boo.*

1128. — a samba. — sambu. — *SAM-boo.*

1129. — a tango. — tango. — *TAN-go.*

1130. — a waltz. — valcer. — *VAL-tser.*

1131. — a folk dance. — narodnu igru. — *NA-rod-noo EE-groo.*

1132. — rock music. — rok muziku. — *rok MOO-zee-koo.*

1133. Discotheque. Diskoteka. *dee-sko-TE-ka.*

SPORTS AND GAMES

1134. We want to play [soccer]. Želimo da igramo [fudbal]. *ZHE-lee-mo da EE-gra-mo [FOOD-bal].*

1135. — basketball. — košarku. — *KO-shar-koo.*

1136. — cards. — karte. — *KAR-te.*

1137. — golf. — golf. — *golf.*

1138. — ping-pong (OR: **table tennis).** — ping-pong (OR: stoni tenis). — *peeng-pong* (OR: *STO-nee TE-nees).*

1139. — tennis. — tenis. — *TE-nees.*

1140. — volleyball. — odbojku. — *OD-boy-koo.*

1141. Do you play [chess]? Igrate li šah? *EE-gra-te lee shah?*

1142. — checkers. — dame. — *DA-me.*

1143. — a bridge. — bridž. — *breedzh.*

1144. Let's go swimming. Hajdemo na plivanje.
HA‿EE-de-mo na PLEE-va-n^y*e.*

1145. Let's go to [the swimming pool].
Hajdemo u [bazen]. *HA‿EE-de-mo oo [BA-zen].*

1146. — the beach. — na plažu. — *na PLA-zhoo.*

1147. — the horse races. — na konjske trke.
— *na KON*^{y}*-ske TŬR-ke.*

1148. — the soccer game. — na fudbalsku utakmicu.
— *na FOOD-bal-skoo OO-tak-mee-tsoo.*

1149. I need [golf equipment]. Treba mi [pribor za golf].
TRE-ba mee [PREE-bor za golf].

1150. — fishing tackle. — pribor za pecanje.
— *PREE-bor za PE-tsa-n*^{y}*e.*

1151. — a tennis racket. — teniska raketa.
— *TE-nee-ska ra-KE-ta.*

1152. Can we go [fishing]?
Možemo li da idemo [na pecanje]?
MO-zhe-mo lee da EE-de-mo [na PE-tsa-n^y*e]?*

1153. — horseback riding. — na jahanje.
— *na YA-ha-n*^{y}*e.*

1154. — roller-skating.
— da se vozimo na rolšuama (w: koturajkama).
— *da se VO-zee-mo na ROL-shoo-a-ma* (w: *ko-TOO-ra‿ee-ka-ma).*

1155. — ice-skating.
— na klizanje na ledu (OR: da se šličugamo).
— *na KLEE-za-n*^{y}*e na LE-doo* (OR: *da se SHLEE-choo-ga-mo).*

1156. —sledding. —na sankanje. —*na SAN-ka-n^{y}e.*

1157. —skiing. —na skijanje. —*na SKEE-ya-n^{y}e.*

HIKING AND CAMPING

1158. How long a walk is it to [the youth hostel]?
Koliko treba da pešačimo do [našeg hostela]?
ko-LEE-ko TRE-ba da pe-SHA-chee-mo do [NA-sheg HO-ste-la]?

1159. Are sanitary facilities available?
Ima li sanitarnih uredjaja?
EE-ma lee SA-nee-tar-neeh OO-re-d^{y}a-ya?

1160. Campsite. Kamping. *KAM-peeng.*

1161. Camping equipment. Pribor za kamping.
PREE-bor za KAM-peeng.

1162. Camping permit. Dozvola za kamping.
DO-zvo-la za KAM-peeng.

1163. Cooking utensils. Pribor za kuvanje.
PREE-bor za KOO-va-n^{y}e.

1164. Firewood. Drva za gorivo.
DŬR-va za GO-ree-vo.

1165. Footpath. Staza. *STA-za.*

1166. Garbage receptacle. Kanta za smeće (OR: djubre).
KAN-ta za SME-t^{y}e (OR: *D^{y}OO-bre).*

1167. Hike. Planinarenje. *pla-nee-NA-re-n^{y}e.*

1168. Matches. Šibice (W: Žigice).
SHEE-bee-tse (W: *ZHEE-gee-tse).*

1169. Picnic. Piknik. *PEEK-neek.*

1170. Shortcut. Preki put (OR: Prečica).
PRE-kee poot (OR: *PRE-chee-tsa).*

1171. Tent. Šator. *SHA-tor.*

1172. Thermos. Termos. *TER-mos.*

1173. Drinking water. Voda za piće (OR: Pijaća voda).
VO-da za PEE-t^{y}e (OR: *PEE-ya-t^{y}a VO-da).*

1174. Forest. Šuma. *SHOO-ma.*

1175. Lake. Jezero. *YE-ze-ro.*

1176. Mountain. Planina (OR: Gora).
PLA-nee-na (OR: *GO-ra).*

1177. River. Reka. *RE-ka.*

1178. Stream. Rečica. *RE-chee-tsa.*

BANK AND MONEY

1179. Where can I change foreign money (LIT.: **currency**) **[at the best rate]?**
Gde mogu da razmenim stranu valutu [po najpovoljnijem kursu]?
gde MO-goo da RAZ-me-neem STRA-noo va-LOO-too [po na‿ee-po-VOL^y-nee-yem KOOR-soo]?

1180. What is the exchange rate on the dollar?
Koji je kurs dolara? *KO-yee ye koors DO-la-ra?*

1181. Will you cash [a personal check] [a traveler's check]?
Da li hoćete da mi unovčite [lični ček] [putnički ček]?
da lee HO-t^{y}e-te da mee oo-NOV-chee-te [LEECH-nee chek] [POOT-neech-kee chek]?

1182. I have [a bank draft] [a letter of credit].
Imam [uplatu čekom] [kreditno pismo].
EE-mam [OO-pla-too CHE-kom] [KRE-deet-no PEE-smo].

1183. I'd like to exchange [twenty] dollars.
Želim da razmenim [dvadeset] dolara.
ZHE-leem da RAZ-me-neem [DVA-de-set] DO-la-ra.

1184. Give me [large bills]. Dajte mi [krupne novčanice].
DA‿EE-te mee [KROOP-ne nov-CHA-nee-tse].

1185. —small bills. —sitne novčanice.
—SEET-ne nov-CHA-nee-tse.

1186. —small change. —sitninu. *—seet-NEE-noo.*

SHOPPING

1187. Show me [the hat] in the window.
Pokažite mi [šešir] u izlogu.
PO-ka-zhee-te mee [SHE-sheer] oo EEZ-lo-goo.

1188. Can you help me? Možete li mi pomoći?
MO-zhe-te lee mee po-MO-t^{y}ee?

1189. I'm just looking around (OR: **browsing).**
Samo razgledam. *SA-mo RAZ-gle-dam.*

1190. I'll come back later. Vratiću se kasnije.
VRA-tee-t^{y}oo se KA-snee-ye.

1191. I've been waiting a long time.
Čekam već dugo. *CHE-kam vet^{y} DOO-go.*

1192. What brand do you have?
Koju vrstu imate? *KO-yoo VŬR-stoo EE-ma-te?*

1193. How much is it [per piece]? Koliko košta [komad]?
ko-LEE-ko KO-shta [KO-mad]?

1194. — per meter. — metar. — *ME-tar.*

1195. — per pound. — funta. — *FOON-ta.*

1196. — per kilo. — kilo. — *KEE-lo.*

1197. — per package. — paketić. — *pa-KE-teet^y^.*

1198. — per bunch. — svežanj. — *SVE-zhan^y^.*

1199. — altogether. — sve skupa. — *sve SKOO-pa.*

1200. It's [too expensive]. To je [suviše skupo].
to ye [SOO-vee-she SKOO-po].

1201. — cheap. — jevtino. — *YEV-tee-no.*

1202. — reasonable. — razumno (OR: pristojno).
— *RA-zoom-no* (OR: *PREE-stoy-no).*

1203. Is that your lowest price?
Je li to vaša najniža cena?
ya lee to VA-sha NA‿EE-nee-zha TSE-na?

1204. Do you give a discount?
Da li dajete sa popustom?
da lee DA-ye-te sa PO-poo-stom?

1205. I [don't] like that. To mi se [ne] dopada.
to mee se [ne] DO-pa-da.

1206. Do you have something [better]?
Imate li nešto [bolje]?
EE-ma-te lee NE-shto [BO-lye]?

1207. — cheaper. — jevtinije. — *YEV-tee-nee-ye.*

1208. — more fashionable. — modernije.
— *mo-DER-nee-ye.*

1209. — softer. — mekše. — *MEK-she.*

1210. — stronger. — jače. — *YA-che.*

1211. — heavier. — teže. — *TE-zhe.*

1212. — lighter (in weight). — lakše. — *LAK-she.*

1213. — tighter. — tešnje. — *TE-shn^{y}e.*

1214. — looser. — šire. *SHEE-re.*

1215. — lighter (in color). — svetlije. — *SVE-tlee-ye.*

1216. — darker. — tamnije. — *TAM-nee-ye.*

1217. Do you have this in [my size]?
Imate li [moj broj]? *EE-ma-te lee [moy broy]?*

1218. — a larger size. — veći broj. — *VE-t^{y}ee broy.*

1219. — a smaller size. — manji broj. — *MA-n^{y}ee broy.*

1220. May I order it in [another color] [a different style]?
Mogu li da naručim u [drugoj boji] [drugom modelu]?
MO-goo lee da NA-roo-cheem oo [DROO-goy BO-yee] [DROO-gom mo-DE-loo]?

1221. Where is the dressing (OR: **fitting) room?**
Gde je kabina za probu?
gde ye ka-BEE-na za PRO-boo?

1222. May I try it on? Mogu li da probam?
MO-goo lee da PRO-bam?

1223. It doesn't fit.
Nije mi taman (OR: Ne pasuje mi, Ne stoji mi dobro).
NEE-ye mee ta-MAN (OR: *ne PA-soo-ye mee, ne STO-yee mee DO-bro).*

1224. Too short. Suviše kratko.
SOO-vee-she KRAT-ko.

1225. Too long. Suviše dugačko.
SOO-vee-she DOO-gach-ko.

1226. Too big. Suviše veliko. *SOO-vee-she VE-lee-ko.*

1227. Too small. Suviše malo. *SOO-vee-she MA-lo.*

1228. Take the measurements. Uzmite meru. *OO-zmee-te ME-roo.*

1229. Length. Dužina. *doo-ZHEE-na.*

1230. Width. Širina. *shee-REE-na.*

1231. This isn't my size. Ovo nije moj broj. *O-vo NEE-ye moy broy.*

1232. I like it. Dopada mi se. *DO-pa-da mee se.*

1233. Have this ready soon. Da ovo bude uskoro gotovo. *da O-vo BOO-de OO-sko-ro GO-to-vo.*

1234. How long will it take to make the alterations?
Koliko dugo treba za popravku?
ko-LEE-ko DOO-go TRE-ba za PO-prav-koo?

1235. Does the price include alterations?
Da li cena uključuje i popravku?
da lee TSE-na oo-KL'OO-choo-ye ee PO-prav-koo?

1236. I can't decide. Ne mogu da se odlučim.
ne MO-goo da se od-LOO-cheem.

1237. I'll wait until it's ready.
Čekaću dok ne bude gotovo.
CHE-ka-t'oo dok ne BOO-de GO-to-vo.

1238. Will it [shrink] [break] [tear]?
Da li će se [skupiti] [slomiti] [pocepati]?
da lee t'e se [SKOO-pee-tee] [SLO-mee-tee] [po-TSE-pa-tee]?

1239. Is it [new]? Je li [novo]? *ye lee [NO-vo]?*

1240. — handmade. — ručni rad. — *ROOCH-nee rad.*

1241. — an antique. — starina (OR: antika).
— *sta-REE-na* (OR: *AN-tee-ka).*

1242. — a replica. — duplikat (OR: kopija).
— *doo-PLEE-kat* (OR: *KO-pee-ya).*

1243. — an imitation. — imitacija.
— *ee-mee-TA-tsee-ya.*

1244. — secondhand. — polovno. — *PO-lov-no.*

1245. Wrap this. Spakujte ovo. *SPA-koo‿ee-te O-vo.*

1246. Where do I pay? Gde treba da platim?
gde TRE-ba da PLA-teem?

1247. Do I pay [the salesman] [the saleswoman]?
Da li da platim [prodavcu] [prodavačici]?
da lee da PLA-teem [pro-DAV-tsoo] [pro-da-VA-chee-tsee]?

1248. Will you honor this credit card?
Da li primate kreditnu kartu?
da lee PREE-ma-te KRE-deet-noo KAR-too?

1249. May I pay with a personal check?
Mogu li da platim ličnim čekom?
MO-goo lee da PLA-teem LEECH-neem CHE-kom?

1250. Is this identification acceptable? (LIT.: **Do you accept** [OR: **honor] this identification?**)
Da li uvažavate ovu ispravu?
da lee oo-va-ZHA-va-te O-voo EE-spra-voo?

1251. Is the reference sufficient?
Da li je podatak dovoljan?
da lee ye po-DA-tak DO-vo-lyan?

1252. Can you send it to my hotel?
Možete li da pošaljete to u moj hotel?
MO-zhe-te lee da PO-sha-l'e-te to oo moy HO-tel?

1253. Can you ship it [to Philadelphia]?
Možete li da pošaljete to [u Filadelfiju]?
MO-zhe-te lee da PO-sha-l^{y}e-te to [oo fee-la-DEl-fee-yoo]?

1254. Pack this carefully for export.
Spakujte ovo pažljivo za izvoz.
SPA-koo‿ee-te O-vo PAZH-l^{y}ee-vo za EEZ-voz.

1255. Give me [a bill]. [Račun] molim vas.
[RA-choon] MO-leem vas.

1256. — a receipt. Priznanicu —.
PREE-zna-nee-tsoo —.

1257. — a credit memo. Odobrenje kredita —.
o-do-BRE-n^{y}e kre-DEE-ta —.

1258. I'll pay upon delivery (LIT.: **when delivered).**
Platiću kad isporučite.
PLA-tee-t^{y}oo kad ee-SPO-roo-chee-te.

1259. Is there an additional charge (LIT.: **Is it necessary to pay additional) for delivery?**
Da li treba da doplatim za isporuku?
da lee TRE-ba da DO-pla-teem za EE-spo-roo-koo?

1260. I'd like to return this article.
Želim da vratim ovu robu.
ZHE-leem da VRA-teem O-voo RO-boo.

1261. Refund (LIT.: **Return) my money.**
Vratite mi moj novac.
VRA-tee-te mee moy NO-vats.

1262. Exchange this. Zamenite ovo.
za-ME-nee-te O-vo.

CLOTHING AND ACCESSORIES

1263. Bathing cap. Kapa za tuširanje.
KA-pa za too-SHEE-ra-n^{y}e.

1264. Bathing suit. Kupaći kostim.
KOO-pa-t^{y}ee KO-steem.

1265. Blouse. Bluza. *BLOO-za.*

1266. Elastic belt. Elastični kaiš.
e-LA-steech-nee KA-eesh.

1267. Boots. Čizme. *CHEEZ-me.*

1268. Bracelet. Narukvica. *NA-rook-vee-tsa.*

1269. Brassiers. Prslučić (OR: Brushalter).
PŬR-sloo-cheet^{y} (OR: *BROOS-hal-ter).*

1270. Briefs (men's). Muške slip-gaćice.
MOO-shke sleep-GA-t^{y}ee-tse.

1271. Button. Dugme. *DOOG-me.*

1272. Cane. Štap. *shtap.*

1273. A cap. Kapa. *KA-pa.*

1274. Coat. Kaput. *KA-poot.*

1275. Collar. Okovratnik. *o-KO-vrat-neek.*

1276. Cufflinks. Dugmeta za manžetne.
doog-ME-ta za man-ZHET-ne.

1277. Dress. Haljina. *HA-l^{y}ee-na.*

1278. Earings. Mindjuše. *MEEN-d^{y}oo-she.*

1279. Pair of gloves. Par rukavica.
par roo-KA-vee-tsa.

1280. Handbag (OR: **Pocketbook).**
Tašna. *TA-shna.*

1281. Handkerchiefs. Maramica (W: Rubac).
MA-ra-mee-tsa (W: *ROO-bats).*

1282. Jacket. Žaket (OR: Jakna).
ZHA-ket (OR: *YAK-na).*

1283. Dinner jacket. Smoking. *SMO-keeng.*

1284. Lingerie. Ženski veš. *ZHEN-skee vesh.*

1285. Necktie. Mašna (OR: Kravata).
MA-shna (OR: *kra-VA-ta).*

1286. Nightgown. Spavaćica. *spa-VA-t^y^ee-tsa.*

1287. Pajamas. Pidžama. *pee-DZHA-ma.*

1288. Panties. Gaćice. *GA-t^y^ee-tse.*

1289. Panty hose (OR: **Tights).**
Hula-hopke. *hoo-la-HOP-ke.*

1290. Parasol. Suncobran. *soon-TSO-bran.*

1291. Decorative pin. Ukrasna igla.
OO-kra-sna EE-gla.

1292. Straight pin. Igla. *EE-gla.*

1293. Safety pin. Zihernadla. *ZEE-her-nad-la.*

1294. Raincoat. Kišni mantil. *KEE-shnee MAN-teel.*

1295. Ribbon. Traka. *TRA-ka.*

1296. Ring. Prsten. *PŬR-sten.*

1297. Rubbers (OR: **Galoshes).** Kaljače.
KA-l^y^a-che.

1298. Sandals. Sandale. *SAN-da-le.*

1299. **Scarf.** Marama. *MA-ra-ma.*

1300. **Shawl.** Šal. *shal.*

1301. **Shirt.** Košulja. *KO-shoo-l^{y}a.*

1302. **Shoelaces.** Pertle. *PERT-le.*

1303. **Shoes.** Cipele. *TSEE-pe-le.*

1304. **Slippers.** Papuče. *PA-poo-che.*

1305. **Socks** (OR: **Stockings**). Čarape. *CHA-ra-pe.*

1306. **Walking shorts (men's).** Kratke pantalone. *KRAT-ke pan-ta-LO-ne.*

1307. **Skirt.** Suknja. *SOOK-n^{y}a.*

1308. **Full slip.** Kombinezon. *kom-bee-NE-zon.*

1309. **Half slip.** Podsuknja. *POD-sook-n^{y}a.*

1310. **Strap.** Kaiš. *KA-eesh.*

1311. **Man's suit.** Odelo. *o-DE-lo.*

1312. **Sweater.** Džemper (OR: Pulover). *DZHEM-per* (OR: *POO-lo-ver).*

1313. **Pair of trousers.** Pantalone (W: Hlače). *pan-ta-LO-ne* (W: *HLA-che).*

1314. **Umbrella.** Kišobran (OR: Amrel). *kee-SHO-bran* (OR: *AM-rel).*

1315. **Undershirt.** Potkošulja. *POT-ko-shoo-l^{y}a.*

1316. **Undershorts.** Muške gaće. *MOO-shke GA-t^{y}e.*

1317. **Underwear.** Donji veš. *DO-n^{y}ee vesh.*

1318. **Wallet.** Novčanik. *nov-CHA-neek.*

COLORS

1319. Black. Crn. *tsŭrn.*

1320. [Light] [Dark] [Medium] blue.
[Svetlo] [Tamno] [Srednje] plav.
[SVET-lo] [TAM-no] [SRED-n^{y}e] plav.

1321. Brown. Smedj (OR: Mrk). *smed^y* (OR: mŭrk).

1322. Gray. Siv (OR: Grao). *seev* (OR: *GRA-o).*

1323. Green. Zelen. *ZE-len.*

1324. Olive green. Maslinast. *MA-slee-nast.*

1325. Orange. Narandžast. *NA-ran-dzhast.*

1326. Pink. Roza. *RO-za.*

1327. Purple. Ljubičast. *L^{y}OO-bee-chast.*

1328. Red. Crven. *TSŬR-ven.*

1329. Tan. Drap. *drap.*

1330. White. Beo. *BE-o.*

1331. Yellow. Žut. *zhoot.*

MATERIALS

1332. Metal. Metal. *ME-tal.*

1333. Aluminum. Aluminijum.
a-loo-MEE-nee-yoom.

1334. Brass. Bronza (OR: Mesing).
BRON-za (OR: *ME-seeng).*

1335. Copper. Bakar. *BA-kar.*

1336. Gold. Zlato. *ZLA-to.*

1337. Iron. Gvoždje. *GVOZH-d*^{y}*e.*

1338. Silver. Srebro. *SRE-bro.*

1339. Steel. Čelik. *CHE-leek.*

1340. Textiles. Tekstil. *TEK-steel.*

1341. Cotton. Pamuk. *PA-mook.*

1342. Dacron. Dakron. *DA-kron.*

1343. Nylon. Najlon. *NA‿EE-lon.*

1344. Orlon. Orlon. *OR-lon.*

1345. Silk. Svila. *SVEE-la.*

1346. Synthetic. Sintetika. *seen-TE-tee-ka.*

1347. Wool. Vuna. *VOO-na.*

1348. Ceramics. Keramika. *ke-RA-mee-ka.*

1349. China. Kineski porculan. *KEE-ne-skee por-TSOO-lan.*

1350. Crystal. Kristal. *KREE-stal.*

1351. Fur. Krzno (OR: Bunda). *KŬR-zno* (OR: *BOON-da).*

1352. Glass. Staklo. *STA-klo.*

1353. Leather. Koža. *KO-zha.*

1354. Plastic. Plastika. *PLA-stee-ka.*

1355. Stone. Kamen. *KA-men.*

1356. Wood. Drvo. *DŬR-vo.*

BOOKSHOP, STATIONER, NEWSDEALER

1357. Do you have [any books] in English?
Imate li [knjige] na engleskom?
EE-ma-te lee [KN^{y}EE-ge] na EN-gle-skom?

1358. Playing cards. Karte za igranje.
KAR-te za EE-gra-n^{y}e.

1359. Dictionary. Rečnik. *RECH-neek.*

1360. A dozen envelopes. Tuce koverata.
TOO-tse KO-ve-ra-ta.

1361. Eraser. Guma za brisanje.
GOO-ma za BREE-sa-n^{y}e.

1362. Fiction. Proza. *PRO-za.*

1363. Folders. Fascikle (OR: Mape).
fas-TSEE-kle (OR: *MA-pe).*

1364. Guidebook. Vodič. *VO-deech.*

1365. Ink. Mastilo (W: Crnilo, Tinta).
MA-stee-lo (W: *TSŬR-nee-lo, TEEN-ta).*

1366. Map. Mapa. *MA-pa.*

1367. Magazines. Časopisi. *CHA-so-pee-see.*

1368. Newspaper. Novine. *NO-vee-ne.*

1369. Nonfiction. Stručne knjige.
STROOCH-ne KN^{y}EE-ge.

1370. Notebook. Beležnica (OR: Blok).
BE-lezh-nee-tsa (OR: *blok).*

1371. Airmail stationery. Hartija za avionska pisma.
HAR-tee-ya za a-VEE-on-ska PEE-sma.

1372. Carbon paper. Indigo. *EEN-dee-go.*

1373. Notepaper. Hartija za beleške.
HAR-tee-ya za BE-le-shke.

1374. Writing paper. Hartija za pisanje.
HAR-tee-ya za PEE-sa-n^y*e.*

1375. Ballpoint pen. Hemijska olovka.
HE-meey-ska O-lov-ka.

1376. Fountain pen. Naliv-pero (OR: Penkalo) (W: Stilo).
NA-leev-pe-ro (OR: *pen-KA-lo)* (W: *STEE-lo).*

1377. Pencil. Olovka. *O-lov-ka.*

1378. Masking tape. Papir za pokrivanje.
PA-peer za po-KREE-va-n^y*e.*

1379. String. Kanap (OR: Konac).
KA-nap (OR: *KO-nats).*

1380. Transparent tape. Selotejp. *SE-lo-teyp.*

1381. Typewriter. Pisaća mašina.
PEE-sa-t^y*a ma-SHEE-na.*

1382. Typewriter ribbon. Vrpca za pisaću mašinu.
VŬRP-tsa za PEE-sa-t^y*oo ma-SHEE-noo.*

1382. Wrapping paper. Papir za pakovanje.
PA-peer za PA-ko-va-n^y*e.*

PHARMACY

1384. Is there [a pharmacy] here where they understand English?
Ima li [apoteka] u kojoj razumeju engleski?
EE-ma lee [a-po-TE-ka] oo KO-yoy ra-ZOO-me-yoo EN-gle-skee?

1385. May I speak to [a male clerk] [a female clerk]?
Mogu li da govorim sa [činovnikom] [činovnicom]?
MO-goo lee da GO-vo-reem sa [chee-NOV-nee-kom] [chee-NOV-nee-tsom]?

1386. Can you fill this prescription [immediately]?
Možete li da mi napravite lek po ovom receptu [odmah]?
MO-zhe-te lee da mee NA-pra-vee-te lek po O-vom RE-tsep-too [OD-mah]?

1387. Is it [mild] [safe]? Da li je [blag] [siguran]?
da lee ye [blag] [SEE-goo-ran]?

1388. Antibiotic. Antibiotik. *an-tee-bee-O-teek.*

1389. Sleeping pill. Pilula za spavanje.
PEE-loo-la za SPA-va-n^{y}e.

1390. Poison. Otrov. *OT-rov.*

1391. Tranquilizer. Sredstvo za umirenje.
SRED-stvo za oo-mee-RE-n^{y}e.

1392. Warning. Opomena (OR: Upozorenje).
O-po-me-na (OR: *oo-po-zo-RE-n^{y}e).*

1393. Take as directed. Uzimati po uputstvu.
oo-ZEE-ma-tee po oo-POOT-stvoo.

1394. Not to be taken internally.
Ne za unutrašnju upotrebu.
ne za OO-noo-tra-shn^{y}oo OO-po-tre-boo.

1395. For external use only.
Samo za spoljnu upotrebu.
SA-mo za SPOL^{y}-noo OO-po-tre-boo.

DRUGSTORE ITEMS

1396. Adhesive bandage. Flaster. *FLA-ster.*

1397. Adhesive tape. Lepljiva traka. *LEP-l^{y}ee-va TRA-ka.*

1398. Alcohol. Alkohol. *AL-ko-hol.*

1399. Antiseptic. Antiseptik. *an-tee-SEP-teek.*

1400. Aspirin (OR: **Analgesic).** Aspirin. *a-SPEE-reen.*

1401. Bandages. Zavoji. *ZA-vo-yee.*

1402. Bath oil. Ulje za kupanje. *OO-l^{y}e za KOO-pa-n^{y}e.*

1403. Bath salts. So za kupanje. *so za KOO-pa-n^{y}e.*

1404. Bicarbonate of soda. Bikarbona soda. *bee-kar-BO-na SO-da.*

1405. Boric acid. Borna kiselina. *BOR-na kee-se-LEE-na.*

1406. Chewing gum. Guma za žvakanje. *GOO-ma za ZHVA-ka-n^{y}e.*

1407. Cleaning fluid. Tečnost za čišćenje. *TECH-nost za CHEESH-t^{y}e-n^{y}e.*

1408. Cleansing tissues. Papirna maramica za lice. *PA-peer-na MA-ra-mee-tsa za LEE-tse.*

1409. Cold cream. Pomada. *po-MA-da.*

1410. Cologne. Kolonjska voda. *ko-LON^{y}-ska VO-da.*

1411. Comb. Češalj. *CHE-shal^{y}.*

1412. **(Powder) compact.** Čvrst puder. *chvrst POO-der.*

1413. **Contraceptives.** Kontraceptivno sredstvo. *kon-tra-TSEP-teev-no SRED-stvo.*

1414. **Corn pad.** Flaster za žuljeve. *FLA-ster za ZHOO-l^y^e-ve.*

1415. **Cotton (absorbent).** Vata. *VA-ta.*

1416. **Cough syrup.** Sirup za kašalj. *SEE-roop za KA-shal^y^.*

1417. **Deodorant.** Deodorans. *de-O-do-rans.*

1418. **Depilatory.** Sredstvo za skidanje dlake. *SRED-stvo za SKEE-da-n^y^e DLA-ke.*

1419. **Disinfectant.** Dezinfekciono sredstvo. *de-zeen-FEK-tsee-o-no SRED-stvo.*

1420. **Earplugs.** Čep za uši. *chep za OO-shee.*

1421. **Enema bag.** Klistir. *KLEE-steer.*

1422. **Epsom salts.** Epsemska so. *EP-sem-ska so.*

1423. **Eye wash** (LIT.: **drops).** Kapi za oči. *KA-pee za O-chee.*

1424. **Gauze.** Gaza. *GA-za.*

1425. **Hairbrush.** Četka za kosu. *CHET-ka za KO-soo.*

1426. **Hair clip** (OR: **Bobby pin).** Šnala. *SHNA-la.*

1427. **Hair net.** Mreža za kosu (OR: Net). *MRE-zha za KO-soo* (OR: *net).*

1428. **Hairpins.** Ukosnica. *OO-ko-snee-tsa.*

1429. **Hair spray.** Sprej (OR: Lak) za kosu. *sprey* (OR: *lak) za KO-soo.*

1430. **Hand lotion.** Pomada za ruke. *po-MA-da za ROO-ke.*

1431. Hot-water bottle. Termofor. *TER-mo-for.*

1432. Ice bag. Kesa za led. *KE-sa za led.*

1433. Insecticide.
Insekticid (OR: Sredstvo za tamanjenje insekata).
in-SEK-tee-tseed (OR: *SRED-stvo za ta-MA-n^{y}e-n^{y}e EEN-se-ka-ta).*

1434. Iodine. Jod. *yod.*

1435. Laxative. Laksativ. *LAK-sa-teev.*

1436. Lipstick. Karmin. *KAR-meen.*

1437. Medicine dropper. Pipeta. *pee-PE-ta.*

1438. Mirror. Ogledalo. *o-GLE-da-lo.*

1439. Mouthwash. Voda za ispiranje usta.
VO-da za ee-SPEE-ra-n^{y}e OO-sta.

1440. Nail file. Turpija za nokte.
TOOR-pee-ya za NOK-te.

1441. Nail polish. Lak za nokte. *lak za NOK-te.*

1442. Nose drops. Kapi za nos. *KA-pee za nos.*

1443. Ointment. Mast. *mast.*

1444. Peroxide. Superoksid. *SOO-per-ok-seed.*

1445. [Face] powder. Puder [za lice].
POO-der [za LEE-tse].

1446. Foot powder. Prašak za noge.
PRA-shak za NO-ge.

1447. Talcum powder. Talk. *talk.*

1448. Powder puff. Pufna. *POOF-na.*

1449. [Straight] [electric] razor.
[Običan] [električni] brijač.
[O-bee-chan] [e-LEK-treech-nee] BREE-yach.

1450. Razor blade (OR: **Safety razor).**
Žilet. *ZHEE-let.*

1451. Rouge. Ruž. *roozh.*

1452. Sanitary napkins. Higijenski ulošci.
hee-GEE-yen-skee OO-losh-tsee.

1453. Sedative. Sredstvo za umirenje.
SRED-stvo za oo-mee-RE-n^{y}e.

1454. Shampoo. Šampon. *SHAM-pon.*

1455. Shaving [brush] [lotion].
[Tečnost] [Četkica] za brijanje.
[TECH-nost] [CHET-kee-tsa] za BREE-ya-n^{y}e.

1456. Shaving cream (brushless). Pasta za brijanje.
PA-sta za BREE-ya-n^{y}e.

1457. Shower cap. Kapa za tuš. *KA-pa za toosh.*

1458. Smelling salts. Mirišljave soli.
mee-REE-shl^{y}a-ve SO-lee.

1459. Sponge. Sundjer. *SOON-d^{y}er.*

1460. Sunburn ointment. Mast za opekotine od sunca.
mast za o-PE-ko-tee-ne od SOON-tsa.

1461. Sunglasses. Naočare za sunce.
NA-o-cha-re za SOON-tse.

1462. Suntan oil (OR: **lotion).** Losion za sunčanje.
lo-SEE-on za SOON-cha-n^{y}e.

1463. Syringe. Brizgalica (OR: Štrcaljka).
*BREE-zga-lee-tsa (*OR: *shtŭr-TSAL^y-ka).*

1464. Tampons. Tamponi. *tam-PO-nee.*

1465. Thermometer. Termometar. *TER-mo-me-tar.*

1466. Toothbrush. Četkica za zube.
CHET-kee-tsa za ZOO-be.

1467. Toothpaste. Pasta za zube (OR: Kalodont).
PA-sta za ZOO-be (OR: *ka-LO-dont).*

1468. Toothpowder. Prašak za zube.
PRA-shak za ZOO-be.

1469. Vaseline. Vazelin. *va-ZE-leen.*

1470. Vitamins. Vitamini. *vee-ta-MEE-nee.*

CAMERA SHOP AND PHOTOGRAPHY

1471. I want a roll of film [for this camera].
Želim jedan film [za ovaj foto-aparat].
ZHE-leem YE-dan feelm [za O-va‿ee fo-to-a-PA-rat].

1472. Do you have [color film]?
Imate li [film u boji]?
EE-ma-te lee [feelm oo BO-yee]?

1473. — black-and-white film. — crno-beli film.
— tsŭr-no-BE-lee feelm.

1474. — movie film. — film za kameru.
— feelm za KA-me-roo.

1475. What is the charge [for developing a roll]?
Koliko košta [razvijanje]?
ko-LEE-ko KO-shta [raz-VEE-ya-nʸe]?

1476. — for enlarging. — uveličavanje.
— oo-ve-lee-CHA-va-nʸe.

1477. — for one print. — jedna slika.
— YED-na SLEE-ka.

1478. May I take a photo of you? Mogu li da vas slikam? *MO-goo lee da vas SLEE-kam?*

1479. Would you take a photo of [me] [us]? Da li biste hteli da [me] [nas] slikate? *da lee BEE-ste HTE-lee da [me] [nas] SLEE-ka-te?*

1480. Battery. Baterija. *BA-te-ree-ya.*

1481. Color print. Slika u boji (OR: koloru). *SLEE-ka oo BO-yee* (OR: *ko-LO-roo).*

1482. Flash cubes. Fleš kockice. *flesh KOTS-kee-tse.*

1483. Electronic flash. Električni fleš. *e-LEK-treech-nee flesh.*

1484. Lens. Sočivo. *SO-chee-vo.*

1485. Negative. Negativ. *NE-ga-teev.*

1486. Slide (OR: **Transparency).** Dijapozitiv. *dee-ya-PO-zee-teev.*

1487. Tripod. Nogare (OR: Stativ). *no-GA-re* (OR: *STA-teev).*

See also "Repairs and Adjustments."

GIFT AND SOUVENIR LIST

1488. Basket. Korpa (OR: Koš). *KOR-pa* (OR: *kosh).*

1489. Box of candy. Kutija bombona. *KOO-tee-ya bom-BO-na.*

1490. Doll. Lutka. *LOOT-ka.*

1491. Embroidery (OR: **Needlework**). Vez. *vez.*

1492. Handicrafts. Ručni radovi.
ROOCH-nee RA-do-vee.

1493. Jewelry. Nakit. *NA-keet.*

1494. Lace. Čipka. *CHEEP-ka.*

1495. Penknife. Džepni nož. *DZHEP-nee nozh.*

1496. Perfume. Miris. *MEE-rees.*

1497. Phonograph records. Gramofonska ploča.
gra-MO-fon-ska PLO-cha.

1498. Pottery. Lončarija (OR: Grnčarija).
lon-CHA-ree-ya (OR: *gŭrn-CHA-ree-ya).*

1499. Precious stone. Dragi kamen.
DRA-gee KA-men.

1500. Print (graphic). Štampana (W: Tiskana) slika.
SHTAM-pa-na (W: *TEE-ska-na) SLEE-ka.*

1501. Reproduction (of a painting, etc.).
Reprodukcija. *re-pro-DOOK-tsee-ya.*

1502. Souvenir. Suvenir (OR: Uspomena).
soo-VE-neer (OR: *OO-spo-me-na).*

1503. Toys. Igračke. *EE-grach-ke.*

TOBACCO STORE

1504. Where is the nearest tobacco store?
Gde je najbliža prodavnica duvana (OR: trafika)?
gde ye NA‿EE-blee-zha PRO-dav-nee-tsa doo-VA-na (OR: *TRA-fee-ka)?*

1505. I want some cigars. Želim nekoliko cigara.
ZHE-leem NE-ko-lee-ko tsee-GA-ra.

1506. Which brands of American cigarettes [with menthol] do you have?
Koje vrste američkih cigareta [sa mentolom] imate?
KO-ye VŬR-ste A-me-reech-keeh tsee-ga-RE-ta [sa MEN-to-lom] EE-ma-te?

1507. One pack of king-size [filter-tip] cigarettes.
Jedno paklo dugačkih cigareta [sa filterom].
YED-no PA-klo DOO-gach-keeh tsee-ga-RE-ta [sa FEEL-te-rom].

1508. I need [a lighter]. Treba mi [upaljač].
TRE-ba mee [oo-PA-lʸach].

1509. —lighter fluid. —benzin za upaljač.
—BEN-zeen za oo-PA-lʸach.

1510. —flint. —kremen. *—KRE-men.*

1511. —matches —šibice. *SHEE-bee-tse.*

1512. —a pipe. —lula. *LOO-la.*

1513. —pipe cleaners. —čistač za lulu.
—CHEE-stach za LOO-loo.

1514. —pipe tobacco. —duvan za lulu.
—DOO-van za LOO-loo.

1515. —a tobacco pouch. —kesa za duvan.
—KE-sa za DOO-van.

LAUNDRY AND DRY CLEANING

1516. Where can I take my laundry to be washed?
Gde mogu da odnesem moje rublje (OR: veš) na pranje?
gde MO-goo da OD-ne-sem MO-ye ROOB-lʸe (OR: *vesh) na PRA-nʸe?*

1517. Is there a dry-cleaning service near here?
Ima li hemijsko čišćenje ovde blizu?
EE-ma lee HE-meey-sko CHEESH-t^{y}e-n^{y}e OV-de BLEE-zoo?

1518. Wash this blouse in [hot water].
Operite ovu bluzu u [vrućoj vodi].
O-pe-ree-te O-voo BLOO-zoo oo [VROO-t^{y}oy VO-dee].

1519. — warm water. — toploj vodi.
— TOP-loy VO-dee.

1520. — lukewarm water. — mlakoj vodi.
— MLA-koy VO-dee.

1521. — cold water. — hladnoj vodi.
— HLAD-noy VO-dee.

1522. No starch. Bez štirka. *bez SHTEER-ka.*

1523. Remove the stain [from this shirt].
Očistite fleku [na ovoj košulji].
O-chee-stee-te FLE-koo [na O-voy KO-shoo-l^{y}ee].

1524. Press [the trousers]. Ispeglajte [pantalone].
ee-SPE-gla‿ee-te [pan-ta-LO-ne].

1525. Starch [the collar]. Uštirkajte [kragnu].
OO-shteer-ka‿ee-te [KRAG-noo].

1526. Dry-clean [this coat].
Dajte [ovaj kaput] na hemijsko čišćenje.
DA‿EE-te [O-va‿ee KA-poot] na HE-meey-sko CHEESH-t^{y}e-n^{y}e.

1527. [The belt] is missing. [Kaiš] nedostaje.
[KA-eesh] ne-DO-sta-ye.

1528. Sew on [this button]. Zašijte [ovo dugme].
ZA-sheey-te [O-vo DOOG-me].

REPAIRS AND ADJUSTMENTS

1529. This doesn't work. Ovo ne radi. *O-vo ne RA-dee.*

1530. This watch is [fast] [slow].
Ovaj sat suviše [ide napred] [zaostaje].
O-va‿ee sat SOO-vee-she [EE-de NA-pred] [za-O-sta-ye].

1531. [My glasses] are broken.
[Moje naočari] su slomljene.
[MO-ye NA-o-cha-ree] soo SLOM-l^{y}e-ne.

1532. It is torn. Pocepalo se. *po-TSE-pa-lo se.*

1533. Where can I get it repaired?
Gde mogu to da popravim?
gde MO-goo to da PO-pra-veem?

1534. Repair [this lock]. Popravite [ovaj katanac].
PO-pra-vee-te [O-va‿ee KA-ta-nats].

1535. Fix [the sole]. Stavite [djon].
STA-vee-te [d^{y}on].

1536. — the heel. — petu. *— PE-too.*

1537. — the uppers. — lice cipele.
— LEE-tse TSEE-pe-le.

1538. — the strap. — kaiš. *— KA-eesh.*

1539. Adjust [this hearing aid].
Podesite [ovaj aparat za gluve].
PO-de-see-te [O-va‿ee a-PA-rat za GLOO-ve].

1540. Lengthen [this skirt]. Produžite [ovu suknju].
pro-DOO-zhee-te [O-voo SOOK-n^{y}oo].

1541. Shorten [the sleeves]. Skratite [rukave].
SKRA-tee-te [roo-KA-ve].

1542. Replace [the lining]. Promenite [postavu].
pro-ME-nee-te [PO-sta-voo].

1543. Mend [the pocket]. Zakrpite [džep].
za-KŬR-pee-te [dzhep].

1544. Fasten it together. Pričvrstite to.
pree-CHVŬR-stee-te to.

1545. Clean [the mechanism]. Očistite [mehanizam].
o-CHEE-stee-te [ME-ha-nee-zam].

1546. Lubricate [the spring]. Podmažite [feder].
POD-ma-zhee-te [FE-der].

1547. Needle. Igla. *EE-gla.*

1548. Scissors. Makaze. *MA-ka-ze.*

1549. Thimble. Naprstak. *NA-pŭr-stak.*

1550. Thread. Konac. *KO-nats.*

BARBER SHOP

1551. A haircut, please. Šišanje, molim vas.
SHEE-sha-n^{y}e, MO-leem vas.

1552. Just a trim. Samo podšišajte malo.
SA-mo POD-shee-sha‿ee-te MA-lo.

1553. (A) shave. Brijanje. *BREE-ya-n^{y}e.*

1554. Shoeshine. Čišćenje cipela.
CHEESH-t^{y}e-n^{y}e TSEE-pe-la.

1555. Don't cut much off [the top].
Nemojte da odsečete suviše [na vrhu].
NE-moy-te da od-SE-che-te SOO-vee-she [na VŬR-hoo].

1556. — the sides. — sa strane. — *sa STRA-ne.*

1557. I want to keep my hair long.
Želim da mi kosa ostane dugačka.
ZHE-leem da mee KO-sa O-sta-ne DOO-gach-ka.

1558. I part my hair [on this side].
Razdeljak je [na ovoj strani].
RAZ-de-l'ak ye [na O-voy STRA-nee].

1559. — on the other side. — na drugoj strani.
— na DROO-goy STRA-nee.

1560. — in the middle. — na sredini.
— na sre-DEE-nee.

1561. No hair tonic. Bez ulja za kosu.
bez OO-l'a za KO-soo.

1562. Trim [my mustache]. Podrežite [moje brkove].
POD-re-zhee-te [MO-ye BŬR-ko-ve].

1563. — my eyebrows. — moje obrve.
— MO-ye O-bŭr-ve.

1564. — my beard. — moju bradu.
— MO-yoo BRA-doo.

1565. — my sideburns. — moje zulufe.
— MO-ye ZOO-loo-fe.

BEAUTY PARLOR

1566. Can I make an appointment for [Monday afternoon]?
Mogu li da zakažem za [ponedeljak po podne]?
MO-goo lee da ZA-ka-zhem za [po-NE-de-l'ak po POD-ne]?

1567. Comb my hair. Očešljajte mi kosu.
O-che-shlʸa‿ee-te mee KO-soo.

1568. Wash my hair. Operite mi kosu.
O-pe-ree-te mee KO-soo.

1569. Shampoo and set. Šamponom i vodenu.
sham-PO-nom ee VO-de-noo.

1570. Not too short. Ne suviše kratko.
ne SOO-vee-she KRAT-ko.

1571. In this style. U ovom stilu.
oo O-vom STEE-loo.

1572. Dye my hair [in this shade].
Ofarbajte mi kosu [ovom bojom].
o-FAR-ba‿ee-te mee KO-soo [O-vom BO-yom].

1573. Clean and set this wig.
Operite i namestite ovu periku.
O-pe-ree-te ee NA-me-stee-te O-voo PE-ree-koo.

1574. Curl. Kovrdža (OR: Lokna).
KO-vŭr-dzha (OR: *LOK-na).*

1575. Facial. Masaža lica. *ma-SA-zha LEE-tsa.*

1576. Hair piece. Perika. *PE-ree-ka.*

1577. Hair rinse (LIT.: **Something to rinse the hair).**
Nešto za ispiranje kose.
NE-shto za ee-SPEE-ra-nʸe KO-se.

1578. Manicure. Manikir. *ma-NEE-keer.*

1579. Massage. Masaža. *ma-SA-zha.*

1580. Permanent wave. Trajna ondulacija.
TRA‿EE-na on-doo-LA-tsee-ya.

STORES AND SERVICES

1581. Antique shop. Antikvarnica.
an-TEE-kvar-nee-tsa.

1582. Art gallery. Umetnička galerija.
OO-met-neech-ka GA-le-ree-ya.

1583. Artist's materials. Umetnički pribor.
OO-met-neech-kee PREE-bor.

1584. Auto rental. Iznajmljivanje kola.
eez-na‿eem-L^{y}EE-va-n^{y}e KO-la.

1585. Auto repairs. Auto-servis. *a-oo-to-SER-vees.*

1586. Bakery. Pekara. *PE-ka-ra.*

1587. Bank. Banka. *BAN-ka.*

1588. Bar. Bar. *bar.*

1589. Barber (OR: **Men's hairdresser).**
Berberin. *BER-be-reen.*

1590. Beauty salon (OR: **Ladies' hairdresser).**
Frizerski salon (OR: Frizerka).
FREE-zer-skee SA-lon (OR: *FREE-zer-ka).*

1591. Bookshop. Knjižara (W: Knjižnica).
KN^{y}EE-zha-ra (W: *KN^{y}EE-zhnee-tsa).*

1592. Butcher shop. Mesarnica. *ME-sar-nee-tsa.*

1593. Candy shop. Prodavnica bombona.
PRO-dav-nee-tsa bom-BO-na.

1594. Checkroom. Garderoba. *gar-de-RO-ba.*

1595. Ladies' clothing. Ženska odeća.
ZHEN-ska O-de-t^{y}a.

1596. Cosmetics. Kozmetika. *koz-ME-tee-ka.*

1597. Dance studio. Škola za igranje.
SHKO-la za EE-gra-n^{y}e.

1598. Delicatessen. Delikatesna radnja.
de-lee-KA-te-sna RAD-n^{y}a.

1599. Dentist. Zubar. *ZOO-bar.*

1600. Department store. Opšta prodavnica.
OP-shta PRO-dav-nee-tsa.

1601. Dressmaker. Krojač (F: Krojačica).
KRO-yach (F: *kro-YA-chee-tsa).*

1602. Drugstore (OR: **Pharmacy).**
Apoteka. *a-po-TE-ka.*

1603. Dry cleaners. Hemijsko čišćenje.
HE-meey-sko CHEESH-t^{y}e-n^{y}e.

1604. Electrical supplies.
Električni pribor (OR: uredjaji).
e-LEK-treech-nee PREE-bor (OR: *OO-re-d^{y}a-yee).*

1605. Employment agency. Biro za zapošljavanje.
BEE-ro za za-po-SHL^{y}A-va-n^{y}e.

1606. Fish store. Prodavnica ribe (W: Ribarnica).
PRO-dav-nee-tsa REE-be (W: *ree-BAR-nee-tsa).*

1607. Florist. Cvećar. *TSVE-t^{y}ar.*

1608. Fruit store.
Voćarnica (OR: Prodavnica voća).
VO-t^{y}ar-nee-tsa (OR: *PRO-dav-nee-tsa VO-t^{y}a).*

1609. Funeral parlor. Pogrebni zavod.
PO-greb-nee ZA-vod.

1610. Furniture store. Radnja nameštaja.
RAD-n^{y}a NA-me-shta-ya.

1611. Gift store. Radnja za poklone.
RAD-n^{y}a za PO-klo-ne.

1612. Grocery. Bakalnica. *BA-kal-nee-tsa.*

1613. Hardware store. Gvoždjarnica.
GVOZH-d^{y}ar-nee-tsa.

1614. Hat shop. Šeširdžinica.
she-SHEER-dzhee-nee-tsa.

1615. Housewares. Kućna roba.
KOOT^{y}-na RO-ba.

1616. Jewelry store. Juvelirska radnja.
yoo-VE-leer-ska RAD-n^{y}a.

1617. Lawyer. Advokat. *ad-VO-kat.*

1618. Laundry.
Servis za pranje rublja (OR: Perionica).
SER-vees za PRA-n^{y}e ROOB-l^{y}a (OR: *pe-ree-O-nee-tsa).*

1619. Loans. Zajmovi. *ZA‿EE-mo-vee.*

1620. Lumberyard. Stovarište dasaka.
STO-va-ree-shte DA-sa-ka.

1621. Market. Pijaca (W: Tržnica).
PEE-ya-tsa (W: *TŬR-zhnee-tsa).*

1622. Money exchange. Menjačnica.
ME-n^{y}ach-nee-tsa.

1623. Music store.
Prodavnica ploča i instrumenata.
PRO-dav-nee-tsa PLO-cha ee een-stroo-ME-na-ta.

1624. Musical instruments. Muzički instrumenti.
MOO-zeech-kee een-stroo-MEN-tee.

1625. Newsstand. Kiosk. *KEE-osk.*

1626. Paints. Boje (OR: Farbe).
BO-ye (OR: *FAR-be).*

1627. Pastry shop.
Poslastičarnica (W: Slastičarnica).
po-sla-STEE-char-neet-sa (W: *sla-STEE-char-nee-tsa).*

1628. Pet shop. Prodavnica životinja. *PRO-dav-nee-tsa zhee-VO-tee-n^{y}a.*

1629. Photographer. Fotograf. *fo-TO-graf.*

1630. Printing. Štamparija. *shtam-PA-ree-ya.*

1631. Real estate. Nekretnine. *ne-kret-NEE-ne.*

1632. Sewing machines. Šivaće mašine. *SHEE-va-t^{y}e ma-SHEE-ne.*

1633. Shoemaker. Obućar. *o-BOO-t^{y}ar.*

1634. Shoe store. Prodavnica obuće. *PRO-dav-nee-tsa O-boo-t^{y}e.*

1635. Sightseeing. Razgledanje znamenitosti. *raz-GLE-da-n^{y}e zna-ME-nee-to-stee.*

1636. Sign painter. Firmopisac. *feer-mo-PEE-sats.*

1637. Sporting goods. Sportska oprema. *SPORT-ska O-pre-ma.*

1638. Stockbroker. Senzal. *SEN-zal.*

1639. Supermarket. Samoposluga (W: Samousluga). *sa-mo-PO-sloo-ga* (W: *sa-mo-OO-sloo-ga).*

1640. Tailor. Krojač (OR: Šnajder). *KRO-yach* (OR: *SHNA‿EE-der).*

1641. Toy shop. Radnja igračaka. *RAD-n^{y}a EE-gra-cha-ka.*

1642. Trucking. Prevoženje kamionima. *PRE-vo-zhe-n^{y}e ka-mee-O-nee-ma.*

1643. Upholsterer. Tapetar. *ta-PE-tar.*

1644. Used cars. Polovna kola. *PO-lov-na KO-la.*

1645. Vegetable store. Prodavnica povrća. *PRO-dav-nee-tsa PO-vŭr-t^{y}a.*

1646. Watchmaker. Sajdžija (W: Urar).
SA‿EE-dzhee-ya (W: *OO-rar).*

1647. Wines and liquors.
Vina i liker (OR: Alkoholna pića).
VEE-na ee LEE-ker (OR: *AL-ko-hol-na PEE-t^{y}a).*

BABY CARE

1648. I need a reliable babysitter (LIT.: **someone reliable to take care of a child) tonight [at 7 o'clock].**
Treba mi neko siguran da mi čuva dete večeras [u sedam sati].
TRE-ba mee NE-ko SEE-goo-ran da mee CHOO-va DE-te ve-CHE-ras [oo SE-dam SA-tee].

1649. Call a pediatrician immediately.
Zovite odmah dečjeg lekara.
ZO-vee-te OD-mah DECH-yeg le-KA-ra.

1650. Diaper the baby. Povijte bebu.
PO-veey-te BE-boo.

1651. Bathe the baby. Okupajte bebu.
o-KOO-pa‿ee-te BE-boo.

1652. Put the baby in the crib for a nap (LIT.: **to take a nap).**
Stavite bebu u krevetac da malo odspava.
STA-vee-te BE-boo oo kre-VE-tats da MA-lo OD-spa-va.

1653. Give the baby a pacifier if he (OR: **she) cries.**
Dajte bebi cuclu ako plače.
DA‿EE-te BE-bee TSOOTS-loo A-ko PLA-che.

1654. Do you have an ointment for diaper rash?
Da li imate mast, ojela se beba?
da lee EE-ma-te mast, O-ye-la se BE-ba?

1655. Take the baby to the park in the carriage (OR: **stroller).**
Odvezite bebu u park u kolicama.
OD-ve-zee-te BE-boo oo park oo ko-LEE-tsa-ma.

1656. Baby food. Hrana za bebe (OR: Dečja hrana).
HRA-na za BE-be (OR: *DECH-ya HRA-na).*

1657. Baby powder. Puder za bebe.
POO-der za BE-be.

1658. Bib. Portikla. *POR-tee-kla.*

1659. Colic. Kolika (OR: Grčevi kod bebe).
KO-lee-ka (OR: *GŬR-che-vee kod BE-be).*

1660. [Disposable bottles] [Disposable (LIT.: **Paper) diapers].**
[Flaše za bacanje] [Papirnate pelene].
[FLA-she za BA-tsa-n^{y}e] [pa-PEER-na-te PE-le-ne].

1661. High chair. Visoka stolica.
VEE-so-ka STO-lee-tsa.

1662. Nursemaid. Dadilja. *DA-dee-l^{y}a.*

1663. Playground. Igralište.
EE-gra-lee-shte.

1664. Rattle. Zvečka. *ZVECH-ka.*

1665. Stuffed toy. Igračka od pliša.
EE-grach-ka od PLEE-sha.

HEALTH AND ILLNESS

1666. Is the doctor [at home] [in the office]?
Da li je doktor [kod kuće] [u ordinaciji]?
da lee ye DOK-tor [kod KOO-t^{y}e] [oo or-dee-NA-tsee-yee]?

1667. What are [his] [her] office hours?
Kad [on] [ona] ordinira? *kad [on] [ona] or-DEE-nee-ra?*

1668. Take [my temperature] [my blood pressure].
Izmerite mi [vatru] [pritisak].
EEZ-me-ree-te mee [VA-troo] [PREE-tee-sak].

1669. I have something in my eye.
Nešto mi je upalo u oko.
NE-shto- mee ye OO-pa-lo oo O-ko.

1670. I have a pain [in my back].
Bole me [ledja]. *BO-le me [LE-d^{y}a].*

1671. [My toe] is swollen. [Prst na nozi] je otekao.
[pŭrst na NO-zee] ye O-te-ka-o.

1672. It's sensitive to pressure (LIT.: **It hurts when pressed).**
Boli kad se pritisne. *BO-lee kad se PREE-tee-sne.*

1673. Is it serious? Da li je ozbiljno?
da lee ye OZ-beel^y-no?

1674. I don't sleep well. Ne spavam dobro.
ne SPA-vam DO-bro.

1675. I have no appetite. Nemam apetit.
NE-mam a-PE-teet.

1676. Can you give me something to relieve the pain?
Možete li mi nešto dati protiv bolova?
MO-zhe-te lee mee NE-shto DA-tee PRO-teev BO-lo-va?

1677. I'm allergic to [penicillin].
Alergičan (F: Alergična) sam na [penicilin].
a-LER-gee-chan (F: *a-LER-gee-chna) sam na [pe-nee-TSEE-leen].*

1678. Where should I have this prescription filled?
Gde mogu da dobijem ovaj lek?
gde MO-goo da DO-bee-yem O-va‿ee lek?

1679. Do I have to go to the hospital?
Treba li da idem u [bolnicu]?
TRE-ba lee da EE-dem oo [BOL-nee-tsoo]?

1680. Is surgery required?
Da li je potrebna operacija?
da lee ye PO-treb-na o-pe-RA-tsee-ya?

1681. Do I have to stay in bed?
Moram li da ležim u krevetu?
MO-ram lee da LE-zheem oo KRE-ve-too?

1682. When will I begin to feel better?
Kad ću početi da se osećam bolje?
kad t^{y}*oo PO-che-tee da se O-se-*t^{y}*am BO-*l^{y}*e?*

1683. Is it contagious? Da li je zarazno?
da lee ye ZA-raz-no?

1684. I feel [better]. Osećam se [bolje].
O-se-t^{y}*am se [BO-*l^{y}*e].*

1685. — worse. — gore. *— GO-re.*

1686. — about the same (way). — otprilike isto.
— ot-PREE-lee-ke EE-sto.

1687. Shall I keep it bandaged?
Treba li da je stalno zavijeno?
TRE-ba lee da ye STAL-no za-VEE-ye-no?

1688. Can I travel [on Monday]?
Smem li da putujem [u ponedeljak]?
smem lee da POO-too-yem [oo po-NE-de-l^{y}ak]?

1689. When will you come again? Kad ćete opet doći?
kad T^{y}E-te O-pet DO-t^{y}ee?

1690. When should I take [the medicine]?
Kad treba da uzmem [lek]?
kad TRE-ba da OO-zmem [lek]?

1691. — the injections. — inekcije. — *ee-NEK-tsee-ye.*

1692. — the pills. — pilule. — *PEE-loo-le.*

1693. Every hour. Svakog sata. *SVA-kog SA-ta.*

1694. [Before] [After] meals. [Pre] [Posle] jela.
[pre] [PO-sle] YE-la.

1695. On going to bed. Pred spavanje.
pred SPA-va-n^{y}e.

1696. On getting up (LIT.: **When you get up).**
Kad ustanete. *kad OO-sta-ne-te.*

1697. Twice a day. Dvaput dnevno.
DVA-poot DNEV-no

1698. Anesthetic. Anestetik. *a-ne-STE-teek.*

1699. Convalescence. Oporavak. *O-po-ra-vak.*

1700. Cure. Lečenje (OR: Ozdravljenje).
LE-che-n^{y}e (OR: *o-zdrav-L^{y}E-n^{y}e).*

1701. Diet. Dijeta. *dee-YE-ta.*

1702. (A) drop. Kap. *kap.*

1703. Nurse. Bolničarka (OR: Nudilja).
BOL-nee-char-ka (OR: *NOO-dee-l^{y}a).*

1704. Ophthalmologist. Očni lekar. *O-chnee LE-kar.*

1705. Orthopedist. Ortoped. *or-TO-ped.*

1706. Remedy. Lek. *lek.*

1707. Specialist. Specijalista. *spe-tsee-YA-lee-sta.*

1708. Surgeon. Hirurg. *HEE-roorg.*

1709. Treatment. Lečenje. *LE-che-n^{y}e.*

1710. X ray. Rendgen. *REND-gen.*

AILMENTS

1711. Abscess. Apsces (OR: Gnojni čir).
AP-stses (OR: *GNOY-nee cheer).*

1712. Allergy. Alergija. *a-LER-gee-ya.*

1713. Appendicitis attack. Napad slepog creva.
NA-pad SLE-pog TSRE-va.

1714. Insect bite. Ubod insekta. *OO-bod EEN-sek-ta.*

1715. Blister. Plik. *pleek.*

1716. Boil. Čir. *cheer.*

1717. Bruise. Modrica. *MO-dree-tsa.*

1718. Burn. Opekotina. *o-PE-ko-tee-na.*

1719. Chicken pox. Srednje (OR: Ovčije) boginje.
SRED-n^{y}e (OR: *OV-chee-ye) BO-gee-n^{y}e.*

1720. Chill. Drhtavica (OR: Jeza).
DŬR-hta-vee-tsa (OR: *YE-za).*

1721. Cold. Nazeb (OR: Prehlada).
NA-zeb (OR: *PRE-hla-da).*

1722. Constipation. Zatvor. *ZAT-vor.*

1723. Corn. Žulj. *zhool^{y}.*

1724. Cough. Kašalj. *KA-shal^{y}.*

1725. Cramp. Grč. *gŭrch.*

1726. Cut. Posekotina. *po-SE-ko-tee-na.*

1727. Diarrhea. Proliv. *PRO-leev.*

1728. Dysentery. Dizenterija. *dee-zen-TE-ree-ya.*

1729. Earache. Uvobolja. *oo-VO-bo-l^{y}a.*

1730. I feel faint. Hvata me nesvestica.
HVA-ta me NE-sve-stee-tsa.

1731. Fever. Groznica (OR: Visoka temperatura).
GRO-znee-tsa (OR: *VEE-so-ka tem-pe-ra-TOO-ra).*

1732. Fracture. Prelom. *PRE-lom.*

1733. Hay fever. Senska groznica.
SEN-ska GRO-znee-tsa.

1734. Headache. Glavobolja. *gla-VO-bo-l^{y}a.*

1735. Indigestion. Nevarenje. *ne-VA-re-n^{y}e.*

1736. Infection. Zaraza. *ZA-ra-za.*

1737. Inflamation. Upala (OR: Zapaljenje).
OO-pa-la (OR: *za-pa-L^{y}E-n^{y}e).*

1738. Influenza. Grip. *greep.*

1739. Insomnia. Nesanica. *ne-SA-nee-tsa.*

1740. Measles.
Male (OR: Dečije) boginje (OR: Rubeola).
MA-le (OR: *DE-chee-ye) BO-gee-n^{y}e* (OR: *roo-be-O-la).*

1741. German measles. Rubela. *roo-BE-la.*

1742. Mumps. Zauške. *ZA-oo-shke.*

1743. Nausea. Muka. *MOO-ka.*

1744. Nosebleed. Krvarenje nosa.
kŭr-VA-re-n^y^e NO-sa.

1745. Pneumonia. Upala pluća. *OO-pa-la PLOO-t^y^a.*

1746. Poisoning. Trovanje. *TRO-va-n^y^e.*

1747. Sore throat. Gušobolja. *goo-SHO-bo-l^y^a.*

1748. Sprain. Istegnuće. *ee-steg-NOO-t^y^e.*

1749. [Bee] sting. Ubod [pčele]. *OO-bod [PCHE-le].*

1750. Sunburn. Opekotina od sunca.
o-PE-ko-tee-na od SOON-tsa.

1751. Swelling. Otok. *O-tok.*

1752. Tonsillitis. Upala krajnika.
OO-pa-la KRA‿EE-nee-ka.

1753. To vomit. Povraćati. *PO-vra-t^y^a-tee.*

See also "Accidents," "Parts of the Body" and "Pharmacy."

DENTIST

1754. Can you recomend [a good dentist]?
Možete li mi preporučiti [dobrog zubara]?
MO-zhe-te lee mee pre-PO-roo-chee-tee [DO-brog zoo-BA-ra]?

1755. I've lost a filling (LIT: **A filling fell out).**
Ispala mi je plomba. *EE-spa-la mee ye PLOM-ba.*

1756. Can you replace [the filling]?
Možete li ponovo staviti [plombu]?
MO-zhe-te lee PO-no-vo STA-vee-tee [PLOM-boo]?

1757. Can you fix [the bridge] [this denture]?
Možete li popraviti [most] [ovu protezu]?
MO-zhe-te lee PO-pra-vee-tee [most] [O-voo pro-TE-zoo]?

1758. This [tooth] hurts me.
Ovaj [zub] me boli. *O-va‿ee [zoob] me BO-lee.*

1759. My gums are sore.
Desni me bole. *DE-snee me BO-le.*

1760. I have a broken tooth (LIT.: **I broke my tooth).**
Slomio (F: Slomila) sam zub.
SLO-mee-o (F: *SLO-mee-la) sam zoob.*

1761. I have a toothache. Boli me zub. *BO-lee me zoob.*

1762. I have a cavity (LIT.: **a rotten tooth).**
Imam pokvaren zub. *EE-mam POK-va-ren zoob.*

1763. Give me [a general anesthetic] [a local anesthetic].
Dajte mi [opštu anesteziju] [lokalnu anesteziju].
DA‿EE-te mee [OP-shtoo a-ne-STE-zee-yoo] [LO-kal-noo a-ne-STE-zee-yoo].

1764. I [don't] want the tooth extracted.
[Ne] želim da mi izvadite zub.
[ne] ZHE-leem da mee EE-zva-dee-te zoob.

1765. A temporary filling.
Privremena plomba. *PREE-vre-me-na PLOM-ba.*

ACCIDENTS

1766. There's been an accident.
Dogodio se nesrećan slučaj.
do-GO-dee-o se NE-sre-tʸan SLOO-cha‿ee.

1767. Get [a doctor] immediately.
Zovite odmah [doktora].
ZO-vee-te OD-mah [DOK-to-ra].

1768. — an ambulance.
— ambulantu (OR: kola za hitnu pomoć).
— am-boo-LAN-too (OR: *KO-la za HEET-noo PO-motʸ).*

1769. — a policeman. — milicajca.
— mee-lee-TSA‿EE-tsa.

1770. He [She] has fallen.
[Pao] [Pala] je. *[PA-o] [PA-la] ye.*

1771. [He] [She] has fainted.
[Onesvestio] [Onesvestila] se.
[o-ne-SVE-stee-o] [o-ne-SVE-stee-la] se.

1772. Don't move [him] [her].
Nemojte [ga] [je] pokretati.
NE-moy-te [ga] [ye] po-KRE-ta-tee.

1773. [My finger] is bleeding.
[Moj prst] krvari. *[moj pŭrst] kŭr-VA-ree.*

1774. A fracture [of the arm]. Prelom [ruke].
PRE-lom [ROO-ke].

1775. I want [to rest] [to sit down] [to lie down].
Želim da [se odmaram] [sednem] [legnem].
ZHE-leem da [se OD-ma-ram] [SED-nem] [LEG-nem].

1776. Notify [my husband] [my wife].
Obavestite [mog muža] [moju ženu].
o-BA-ve-stee-te [mog MOO-zha] [MO-yoo ZHE-noo].

1777. Tourniquet. Naprava za stezanje žila.
NA-pra-va za STE-za-n^{y}e ZHEE-la.

PARTS OF THE BODY

1778. Ankle. Članak. *CHLA-nak.*

1779. Appendix. Slepo crevo. *SLE-po TSRE-vo.*

1780. Arm. Ruka. *ROO-ka.*

1781. Armpit. Pazuho. *PA-zoo-ho.*

1782. Artery. Vena (OR: Arterija).
VE-na (OR: *ar-TE-ree-ya).*

1783. Back. Ledja. *LE-d^{y}a.*

1784. Belly. Stomak. *STO-mak.*

1785. Blood. Krv. *kŭrv.*

1786. Blood vessel. Krvni sud. *KŬRV-nee sood.*

1787. Body. Telo. *TE-lo.*

1788. Bone. Kost. *kost.*

1789. Bowel. Creva. *TSRE-va.*

1790. Brain. Mozak. *MO-zak.*

1791. Breast (OR: **Chest**). Grudi (OR: Prsa).
GROO-dee (OR: *PŬR-sa).*

1792. Calf. List. *leest.*

1793. Cheek. Obraz. *O-braz.*

1794. Chin. Brada. *BRA-da.*

1795. Collarbone. Ključna kost. *KL'OOCH-na kost.*

1796. Ear. Uvo (w: Uho). *OO-vo* (w: *OO-ho).*

1797. Elbow. Lakat. *LA-kat.*

1798. Eye. Oko. *O-ko.*

1799. Eyelashes. Trepavice. *TRE-pa-vee-tse.*

1800. Eyelid. Očni kapak. *OCH-nee KA-pak.*

1801. Face. Lice. *LEE-tse.*

1802. Finger. Prst. *pŭrst.*

1803. Fingernail. Nokat. *NO-kat.*

1804. Foot. Stopalo (OR: Noga). *STO-pa-lo* (OR: *NO-ga).*

1805. Forehead. Čelo. *CHE-lo.*

1806. Gall bladder. Žučna kesica. *ZHOOCH-na KE-see-tsa.*

1807. Genitals. Polni udovi (OR: organi). *POL-nee OO-do-vee* (OR: *or-GA-nee).*

1808. Glands. Žlezde. *ZHLE-zde.*

1809. Gums. Desni. *DE-snee.*

1810. Hair. Kosa. *KO-sa.*

1811. Hand. Ruka. *ROO-ka.*

1812. Head. Glava. *GLA-va.*

1813. Heart. Srce. *SŬR-tse.*

1814. Heel. Peta. *PE-ta.*

1815. Hip. Kuk. *kook.*

1816. Intestines. Creva. *TSRE-va.*

1817. Jaw. Vilica. *VEE-lee-tsa.*

1818. Joint. Zglavak (OR: Članak). *ZGLA-vak* (OR: *CHLA-nak).*

1819. Kidney. Bubreg. *BOO-breg.*

1820. Knee. Koleno. *KO-le-no.*

1821. Larynx. Grkljan. *GŬRK-*l^y*an.*

1822. Leg. Noga. *NO-ga.*

1823. Lip. Usna. *OO-sna.*

1824. Liver. Džigerica (OR: Jetra). *DZHEE-ge-ree-tsa* (OR: *YE-tra).*

1825. Lungs. Pluća. *PLOO-*t^y*a.*

1826. Mouth. Usta. *OO-sta.*

1827. Muscle. Mišić. *MEE-shee*t^y*.*

1828. Navel. Pupak. *POO-pak.*

1829. Neck. Vrat. *vrat.*

1830. Nerve. Živac. *ZHEE-vats.*

1831. Nose. Nos. *nos.*

1832. Pancreas. Gušterača (OR: Pankreas). *goo-SHTE-ra-cha* (OR: *PAN-kre-as).*

1833. Rib. Rebro. *RE-bro.*

1834. Shoulder. Rame. *RA-me.*

1835. Side. Strana (OR: Bok). *STRA-na* (OR: *bok).*

1836. Skin. Koža. *KO-zha.*

1837. Skull. Lobanja. *LO-ba-*n^y*a.*

1838. Spine. Kičma. *KEECH-ma.*

1839. Spleen. Slezina. *SLE-zee-na.*

1840. Stomach. Stomak. *STO-mak.*

1841. Temple. Slepoočnica. *sle-po-OCH-nee-tsa.*

1842. Thigh. Butina. *BOO-tee-na.*

1843. Throat. Grlo. *GŬR-lo.*

1844. Thumb. Palac. *PA-lats.*

1845. Toe. Prst na nozi. *pŭrst na NO-zee.*

1846. Tongue. Jezik. *YE-zeek.*

1847. Tonsils. Krajnici. *KRA‿EE-nee-tsee.*

1848. Vein. Vena. *VE-na.*

1849. Waist. Pojas (OR: Struk). *PO-yas* (OR: *strook).*

1850. Wrist. Ručni zglavak (OR: zglob). *ROOCH-nee ZGLA-vak* (OR: *zglob).*

TIME

1851. What time is it?
Koliko je sati? *ko-LEE-ko ye SA-tee?*

1852. Two A.M. (LIT.: in the morning).
Dva ujutru. *dva OO-yoo-troo.*

1853. Two P.M. (LIT.: in the afternoon).
Dva po podne. *dva po POD-ne.*

1854. It's exactly half-past three (LIT.: half of four).
Tačno pola četiri. *TACH-no PO-la CHE-tee-ree.*

1855. Quarter-past four. Četiri i četvrt. *CHE-tee-ree ee CHET-vŭrt.*

1856. Quarter to five. Četvrt do pet.
CHET-vŭrt do pet.

1857. At ten minutes to six. U deset do šest.
oo DE-set do shest.

1858. At twenty minutes past seven.
U sedam i dvadeset. *oo SE-dam ee DVA-de-set.*

1859. It's early. Rano je. *RA-no ye.*

1860. It's late. Kasno je. *KA-sno ye.*

1861. In the morning. Ujutru. *OO-yoo-troo.*

1862. This afternoon. Danas po podne.
DA-nas po POD-ne.

1863. Tomorrow. Sutra. *SOO-tra.*

1864. In the evening. Uveče. *OO-ve-che.*

1865. At noon. U podne. *oo POD-ne.*

1866. Midnight. Ponoć. *PO-not*^{y}.

1867. During the day.
Preko dana (OR: U toku dana).
PRE-ko DA-na (OR: *oo TO-koo DA-na).*

1868. Every night. Svake noći. *SVA-ke NO-t*^{y}*ee.*

1869. All night. Celu noć. *TSE-loo not*^{y}.

1870. Since yesterday. Od juče. *od YOO-che.*

1871. Today. Danas. *DA-nas.*

1872. Tonight. Noćas. *NO-t*^{y}*as.*

1873. Last month. Prošlog meseca.
PRO-shlog ME-se-tsa.

1874. Last year. Prošle godine. *PRO-shle GO-dee-ne.*

1875. Next Sunday. Iduće nedelje.
EE-doo-t'e NE-de-l'e.

1876. Next week.
Iduće nedelje (OR: sedmice) (W: tjedna).
EE-doo-t'e NE-de-l'e (OR: *SED-mee-tse)* (W: *T'ED-na).*

1877. The day before yesterday.
Prekjuče. *PREK-yoo-che.*

1878. The day after tomorrow.
Prekosutra. *PRE-ko-soo-tra.*

1879. Two weeks ago. Pre dve nedelje (OR: sedmice).
pre dve NE-de-l'e (OR: *SED-mee-tse).*

WEATHER

1880. How's the weather today?
Kakvo je danas vreme? *KAK-vo ye DA-nas VRE-me?*

1881. It looks like rain.
Izgleda da će kiša. *EEZ-gle-da da t'e KEE-sha.*

1882. It's [cold]. [Hladno] je. *[HLAD-no] ye.*

1883. —fair. Lepo —. *LE-po —.*

1884. —warm. Toplo —. *TO-plo —.*

1885. —windy. Vetrovito —. *ve-TRO-vee-to —.*

1886. The weather is clearing. Vreme se prolepšava.
VRE-me se pro-LEP-sha-va.

1887. What a beautiful day!
Kakav lep dan! *KA-kav lep dan!*

1888. I want to sit [in the shade].
Želim da sedim [u hladu].
ZHE-leem da SE-deem [oo HLA-doo].

1889. — in the sun.
— na suncu. *— na SOON-tsoo.*

1890. — in a breeze. — na povetarcu.
— na po-ve-TAR-tsoo.

1891. What is the weather forecast [for tomorrow] [for the weekend]?
Kakva je prognoza [za sutra] [za vikend]?
KAK-va ye prog-NO-za [za SOO-tra] [za VEE-kend]?

1892. It will snow (LIT.: **Snow will fall) tomorrow.**
Sutra će padati sneg. *SOO-tra t^y^e PA-da-tee sneg.*

DAYS OF THE WEEK

1893. Sunday. Nedelja. *NE-de-l^y^a.*

1894. Monday. Ponedeljak. *po-NE-de-l^y^ak.*

1895. Tuesday. Utorak. *OO-to-rak.*

1896. Wednesday. Sreda. *SRE-da.*

1897. Thursday. Četvrtak. *chet-VŬR-tak.*

1898. Friday. Petak. *PE-tak.*

1899. Saturday. Subota. *SOO-bo-ta.*

HOLIDAYS

1900. May first. Prvi maj. *PŬR-vee ma‿ee.*

1901. Merry Christmas.
Srećan Božić (OR: Hristos se rodi).
SRE-t^{y}an BO-zheet^y (OR: *HREE-stos se RO-dee).*

1902. Happy Easter.
Srećan Uskrs (OR: Hristos voskrese).
SRE-t^{y}an OO-skŭrs (OR: *HREE-stos vo-SKRE-se).*

1903. Happy New Year. Srećna Nova godina.
SRE-t^{y}na NO-va GO-dee-na.

1904. Happy birthday. Srećan rodjendan.
SRE-t^{y}an RO-d^{y}en-dan.

1905. Happy anniversary. Srećna godišnjica.
SRE-t^{y}na GO-dee-shn^{y}ee-tsa.

1906. Religious holiday. Verski praznik.
VER-skee PRA-zneek.

1907. State holiday. Državni praznik.
DŬR-zhav-nee PRA-zneek.

DATES, MONTHS AND SEASONS

1908. January. Januar (W: Siječanj).
YA-noo-ar (W: *see-YE-chan^y).*

1909. February. Februar (W: Veljača).
FE-broo-ar (W: *VE-l^{y}a-cha).*

1910. March. Mart (W: Ožujak). *mart* (W: *O-zhoo-yak).*

1911. April. April (w: Travanj).
A-preel (w: *TRA-van*^{y}*)*.

1912. May. Maj (w: Svibanj). *ma‿ee* (w: *SVEE-ban*^{y}*)*.

1913. June. Jun (w: Lipanj). *yoon* (w: *LEE-pan*^{y}*)*.

1914. July. Jul (w: Srpanj). *yool* (w: *SŬR-pan*^{y}*)*.

1915. August. Avgust (w: Kolovoz).
AV-goost (w: *KO-lo-voz)*.

1916. September. Septembar (w: Rujan).
SEP-tem-bar (w: *ROO-yan)*.

1917. October. Oktobar (w: Listopad).
OK-to-bar (w: *LEE-sto-pad)*.

1918. November. Novembar (w: Studeni).
NO-vem-bar (w: *STOO-de-nee)*.

1919. December. Decembar (w: Prosinac).
DE-tsem-bar (w: *PRO-see-nats)*.

1920. Spring. Proleće. *PRO-le-t*^{y}*e*.

1921. Summer. Leto. *LE-to*.

1922. Autumn (OR: **Fall**). Jesen. *YE-sen*.

1923. Winter. Zima. *ZEE-ma*.

1924. Today is the 31st of May, 1987.
Danas je trideset prvi maj hiljadu (w: tisuću) devetsto osamdeset sedme godine.
DA-nas ye TREE-de-set PŬR-vee ma‿ee HEE-l^{y}*a-doo* (w: *TEE-soo-t*^{y}*oo) DE-vet-sto o-sam-DE-set SED-me GO-dee-ne*.

NUMBERS: CARDINALS

1925. Zero. Nula. *NOO-la.*

1926. One. Jedan.* *YE-dan.*

1927. Two. Dva.† *dva.*

1928. Three. Tri. *tree.*

1929. Four. Četiri. *CHE-tee-ree.*

1930. Five. Pet. *pet.*

1931. Six. Šest. *shest.*

1932. Seven. Sedam. *SE-dam.*

1933. Eight. Osam. *O-sam.*

1934. Nine. Devet. *DE-vet.*

1935. Ten. Deset. *DE-set.*

1936. Eleven. Jedanaest. *ye-DA-na-est.*

1937. Twelve. Dvanaest. *DVA-na-est.*

1938. Thirteen. Trinaest. *TREE-na-est.*

1939. Fourteen. Četrnaest. *che-TŬR-na-est.*

1940. Fifteen. Petnaest. *PET-na-est.*

1941. Sixteen. Šesnaest. *SHE-sna-est.*

* You will also see the word for "one" (alone and in numbers ending in "-one," e.g., "twenty-one," "five hundred ninety-one") appearing as Jedna (*YED-na*) and Jedno (*YED-no*).

† You will also see the word for "two" (alone and in numbers ending in "-two," e.g., "fifty-two," "three hundred thirty-two") appearing as Dve (*dve*).

1942. Seventeen. Sedamnaest. *se-DAM-na-est.*

1943. Eighteen. Osamnaest. *o-SAM-na-est.*

1944. Nineteen. Devetnaest. *de-VET-na-est.*

1945. Twenty. Dvadeset. *DVA-de-set.*

1946. Twenty-one. Dvadeset jedan. *DVA-de-set YE-dan.*

1947. Twenty-five. Dvadeset pet. *DVA-de-set pet.*

1948. Thirty. Trideset. *TREE-de-set.*

1949. Forty. Četrdeset. *che-tŭr-DE-set.*

1950. Fifty. Pedeset. *pe-DE-set.*

1951. Sixty. Šezdeset. *shez-DE-set.*

1952. Seventy. Sedamdeset. *se-dam-DE-set.*

1953. Eighty. Osamdeset. *o-sam-DE-set.*

1954. Ninety. Devedeset. *de-ve-DE-set.*

1955. One hundred. Sto. *sto.*

1956. One hundred and one. Sto jedan. *sto YE-dan.*

1957. One hundred and ten. Sto deset. *sto DE-set.*

1958. One thousand. Hiljada (w: Tisuća). *HEE-l^{y}a-da* (w: *TEE-soo-t^{y}a).*

1959. Two thousand. Dve hiljade (w: tisuće). *dve HEE-l^{y}a-de* (w: *TEE-soo-t^{y}e).*

1960. Three thousand. Tri hiljade (w: tisuće). *tree HEE-l^{y}a-de* (w: *TEE-soo-t^{y}e).*

1961. Five thousand. Pet hiljada (w: tisuća). *pet HEE-l^{y}a-da* (w: *TEE-soo-t^{y}a).*

1962. One hundred thousand. Sto hiljada (w: tisuća). *sto HEE-l^{y}a-da* (w: *TEE-soo-t^{y}a).*

1963. One million. Milion (w: Milijun). *mee-LEE-on* (w: *mee-LEE-yoon).*

1964. One billion. Milijarda. *mee-lee-YAR-da.*

NUMBERS: ORDINALS

1965. First. Prvi.* *PŬR-vee.*

1966. Second. Drugi. *DROO-gee.*

1967. Third. Treći. *TRE-t^y^ee.*

1968. Fourth. Četvrti. *CHET-vŭr-tee.*

1969. Fifth. Peti. *PE-tee.*

1970. Sixth. Šesti. *SHE-stee.*

1971. Seventh. Sedmi. *SED-mee.*

1972. Eighth. Osmi. *O-smee.*

1973. Ninth. Deveti. *DE-ve-tee.*

1974. Tenth. Deseti. *DE-se-tee.*

1975. Twentieth. Dvadeseti. *DVA-de-se-tee.*

1976. Thirtieth. Trideseti. *TREE-de-se-tee.*

1977. Hundredth. Stoti. *STO-tee.*

1978. Thousandth. Hiljaditi (w: Tisući). *HEE-l^y^a-dee-tee* (w: *TEE-soo-t^y^ee).*

* In addition to the-*i* ending shown here, ordinal numbers may also take the endings -*a* or -*o*, depending on the noun that follows.

1979. Millionth. Milioniti (W: Milijuniti). *mee-lee-O-nee-tee* (W: *mee-lee-YOO-nee-tee).*

QUANTITIES

1980. A fraction. Razlomak. *RAZ-lo-mak.*

1981. One-quarter. Četvrtina. *chet-vŭr-TEE-na.*

1982. One third. Trećina. *tre-T'EE-na.*

1983. One-half. Polovina. *po-LO-vee-na.*

1984. Three-quarters. Tri četvrtine. *tree chet-vŭr-TEE-ne.*

1985. The whole. Celina. *tse-LEE-na.*

1986. A few. Malo. *MA-lo.*

1987. Several. Nekoliko. *NE-ko-lee-ko.*

1988. Many. Mnogo. *MNO-go.*

FAMILY

1989. Wife. Žena (OR: Supruga). *ZHE-na* (OR: *SOO-proo-ga).*

1990. Husband. Muž (OR: Suprug). *moozh* (OR: *SOO-proog).*

1991. Mother. Majka (OR: Mati). *MA‿EE-ka* (OR: *MA-tee).*

1992. Father. Otac. *O-tats.*

1993. Grandmother. Baba. *BA-ba.*

1994. Grandfather.
Ded (OR: Deda) *ded* (OR: *DE-da).*

1995. Daughter.
Ćerka (OR: Kćer). *T^{y}ER-ka* (OR: *kt^{y}er).*

1996. Son. Sin. *seen.*

1997. Sister. Sestra. *SE-stra.*

1998. Brother. Brat. *brat.*

1999. Aunt. Tetka (OR: Ujna). *TET-ka* (OR: *OOY-na).*

2000. Uncle. Ujak (OR: Stric). *OO-yak* (OR: *streets).*

2001. Niece. Nećaka.* *NE-t^{y}a-ka.*

2002. Nephew. Nećak.† *NE-t^{y}ak.*

2003. Cousin.
Brat (F: Sestra) od tetke (OR: strica, ujaka).
brat (F: *SE-stra) od TET-ke* (OR: *STREE-tsa, OO-ya-ka).*

2004. Relative.
Rodjak (F: Rodjaka). *RO-d^{y}ak* (F: *RO-d^{y}a-ka).*

* In Serbo-Croatian, nećaka means "niece" in general. Other words for "niece" have more specific meanings. Use sinovica (*see-NO-vee-tsa*) or bratanica (*bra-TA-nee-tsa*) to mean "brother's daughter"; use sestričina (*SE-stree-chee-na*) to mean "sister's daughter."

† In Serbo-Croatian, nećak means "nephew" in general. Other words for "nephew" have more specific meanings. Use sinovac (*see-NO-vats*) or bratanac (*bra-TA-nats*) to mean "brother's son"; use sestrić (*SE-street^y*) to mean "sister's son."

2005. Father-in-law.
Svekar (OR: Tast). *SVE-kar* (OR: *tast).*

2006. Mother-in-law.
Svekrva (OR: Tašta). *SVE-kŭr-va* (OR: *TA-shta).*

2007. Adults. Odrasli. *OD-ra-slee.*

2008. Children. Deca. *DE-tsa.*

COMMON SIGNS AND PUBLIC NOTICES

For ease of reference this section is alphabetized according to the Serbo-Croatian entries.

2009. Autobuska stanica.
a-oo-TO-boo-ska STA-nee-tsa.
Bus stop.

2010. Besplatno. *BE-splat-no.*
Free (OR: No charge).

2011. Biblioteka. *bee-blee-o-TE-ka.* Library.

2012. Biletarnica (W). *bee-LE-tar-nee-tsa.*
Ticket office.

2013. Blagajna. *BLA-ga‿ee-na.* Ticket office.

2014. Bolnica. *BOL-nee-tsa.* Hospital.

2015. Čekaonica. *che-KA-o-nee-tsa.* Waiting room.

2016. Čuvaj se psa. *CHOO-va‿ee se psa.*
Beware of dog.

2017. Dobar pazar. *DO-bar PA-zar.* Bargain.

2018. Dole. *DO-le.* Down.

2019. Er kondišn. *er kon-DEE-shn.* Air-conditioned.

2020. Fabrika. *FA-bree-ka.* Factory.

2021. Groblje. *GRO-bl^{y}e.* Cemetery.

2022. Guraj. *GOO-ra‿ee.* Push.

2023. Hladna pića. *HLAD-na PEE-t^{y}a.* Refreshments.

2024. Hladno. *HLAD-no.* Cold.

2025. Informacija. *een-for-MA-tsee-ya.* Information.

2026. Izlaz. *EEZ-laz.* Exit.

2027. Izlaz u slučaju opasnosti. *EEZ-laz oo SLOO-cha-yoo o-PA-sno-stee.* Emergency exit.

2028. Javna govornica. *YAV-na GO-vor-nee-tsa.* Public telephone.

2029. Javna objava. *YAV-na OB-ya-va.* Public notice.

2030. Javno saopštenje. *YAV-no sa-op-SHTE-n^{y}e.* Public notice.

2031. Kasa. *KA-sa.* Ticket office.

2032. Klima uredjaj. *KLEE-ma OO-re-d^{y}a‿ee.* Air conditioned.

2033. Klinika. *KLEE-nee-ka.* Clinic.

2034. Kuća za izdavanje. *KOO-t^{y}a za eez-DA-va-n^{y}e.* House for rent.

2035. Kućepazitelj. *koo-t^{y}e-PA-zee-tel^y.* Janitor.

2036. Lift. *leeft.* Elevator.

2037. Milicija. *MEE-lee-tsee-ya.* Police.

2038. Nagore. *NA-go-re.* Up.

2039. Na desno. *na DE-sno.* To the right.

2040. Na levo. *na LE-vo.* To the left.

2041. Nameštena soba pod najam (OR: **kiriju).**
NA-me-shte-na SO-ba pod NA-yam (OR: *KEE-ree-yoo).*
Furnished rooms for rent.

2042. Na prodaji ovde. *na PRO-da-yee OV-de.*
For sale here.

2043. Na prodaju. *na PRO-da-yoo.* For sale.

2044. Ne hrani životinje. *ne HRA-nee zhee-VO-tee-n^{y}e.*
Do not feed the animals.

2045. Nema predstave. *NE-ma PRED-sta-ve.*
No performance.

2046. Nizbrdo. *NEEZ-bŭr-do.* Downhill.

2047. Non-stop predstava. *non-STOP PRED-sta-va.*
Continuous performance.

2048. Objave. *OB-ya-ve.* Notices.

2049. Odlazak. *OD-la-zak.* Departure.

2050. Opasnost. *o-PA-snost.* Danger.

2051. Opomena. *O-po-me-na.* Warning.

2052. Opština. *OP-shtee-na.* City hall.

2053. Otpaci. *OT-pa-tsee.* Refuse (OR: Garbage).

2054. Otvoreno. *OT-vo-re-no.* Open.

2055. Otvoreno od devet ujutru do osam uveče.
OT-vo-re-no od DE-vet OO-yoo-troo do O-sam OO-ve-che.
Open from 9 A.M. to 8 P.M.

2056. Pazi kako ideš. *PA-zee KA-ko EE-desh.* Watch your step.

2057. Pažnja. *PA-zhn^{y}a.* Attention.

2058. Pažnja radi se. *PA-zhn^{y}a RA-dee se.* Men at work.

2059. Pogodba. *PO-god-ba.* Bargain.

2060. Poštansko sandučе. *PO-shtan-sko SAN-doo-che.* Mail box.

2061. Pozor (W). *PO-zor.* Attention.

2062. Prazno. *PRA-zno.* Vacant (OR: Free).

2063. Privatan put. *PREE-va-tan poot.* Private road.

2064. Privatna svojina. *PREE-vat-na svo-YEE-na.* Private property.

2065. Prodaja. *PRO-da-ya.* Sale.

2066. Prodaja na malo. *Pro-da-ya na MA-lo.* Retail.

2067. Prodaja na veliko. *PRO-da-ya na VE-lee-ko.* Wholesale.

2068. Rasprodaja. *RAS-pro-da-ya.* Sale.

2069. Rezervisano. *re-ZER-vee-sa-no.* Reserved.

2070. Ručak. *ROO-chak.* Lunch.

2071. Samousluga. *sa-mo-OO-sloo-ga.* Self-service.

2072. [Samo] za pešake. *[SA-mo] za pe-SHA-ke.* Pedestrians [only].

2073. Samo za službenike. *SA-mo za SLOOZH-be-nee-ke.* Employees only.

2074. Slobodno. *SLO-bod-no.* Enter (OR: Free).

2075. Služben ulaz. *SLOOZH-ben OO-laz.* Employees only (LIT.: Employees' entrance).

2076. Soba za ručavanje. *SO-ba za roo-CHA-va-n^{y}e.* Dining room.

2077. Stepenice. *STE-pe-nee-tse.* Stairs.

2078. Sveže farbano. *SVE-zhe FAR-ba-no.* Fresh paint (LIT.: Freshly painted).

2079. Taksi stanica. *TAK-see STA-nee-tsa.* Taxi stand.

2080. Telefon. *te-LE-fon.* Telefon.

2081. Televizija. *te-le-VEE-zee-ya.* Television.

2082. Tišina. *tee-SHEE-na.* Quiet (OR: Silence).

2083. Toalet. *to-A-let.* Toilet.

2084. Trgovačka škola. *TŬR-go-vach-ka SHKO-la.* Business school.

2085. Tvornica (W). *TVOR-nee-tsa.* Factory.

2086. Udji. *OO-d^{y}ee.* Enter.

2087. Ulaz. *OO-laz.* Admission (OR: Entrance).

2088. Ulaz besplatan. *OO-laz BE-spla-tan.* Admission free.

2089. Vagon za pušenje. *VA-gon za POO-she-n^{y}e.* Smoking car (OR: Smoker).

2090. Vagon za ručavanje. *VA-gon za roo-CHA-va-n^{y}e.* Dining car.

2091. Vozovi. *VO-zo-vee.* To the trains.

2092. Vraćam se u [jedan po podne (OR: **trinaest)].**
VRA-t^{y}am se oo [YE-dan po POD-ne (OR: *TREE-na-est)].*
Will return at [1 P.M.].

2093. Vrelo. *VRE-lo.* Hot.

2094. Vruće. *VROO-t^{y}e.* Hot.

2095. Vuci. *VOO-tsee.* Pull.

2096. WC. *VE-tse.* Toilet.

2097. Zabranjeno. *ZA-bra-n^{y}e-no.* Forbidden.

2098. Zabranjeno hodati po travi.
ZA-bra-n^{y}e-no HO-da-tee po TRA-vee.
Keep off the grass.

2099. Zabranjeno kupanje. *ZA-bra-n^{y}e-no KOO-pa-n^{y}e.*
Bathing not allowed (OR: No swimming).

2100. Zabranjeno lepljenje plakata.
ZA-bra-n^{y}e-no LEP-l^{y}e-n^{y}e pla-KA-ta.
Post no bills.

2101. Zabranjeno plivanje.
ZA-bra-n^{y}e-no PLEE-va-n^{y}e.
No swimming.

2102. Zabranjeno pljuvanje po podu.
ZA-bra-n^{y}e-no PL^{y}OO-va-n^{y}e po PO-doo.
No spitting.

2103. Zabranjeno pušenje. *ZA-bra-n^{y}e-no POO-she-n^{y}e.*
No smoking.

2104. Zabranjen pristup [osim poslovno].
ZA-bra-n^{y}en PREE-stoop [O-seem PO-slov-no].
No admittance [except on business].

2105. Zabranjen prolaz. *ZA-bra-n^{y}en PRO-laz.*
No trespassing.

2106. Za iznajmljivanje. *za eez-na‿eem-L^{y}EE-va-n^{y}e.* For rent (OR: hire).

2107. Za muškarce. *za moo-SHKAR-tse.* Gentlemen (OR: Men's room).

2108. Zatvoreno nedeljom i praznikom. *ZAT-vo-re-no NE-de-l^{y}om ee PRA-znee-kom.* Closed on Sundays and holidays.

2109. Zatvoreno od osam uveče (OR: **dvadeset) do devet ujutru.** *ZAT-vo-re-no od O-sam OO-ve-che* (OR: *DVA-de-set) do DE-vet OO-yoo-troo.* Closed from 8 P.M. to 9 A.M.

2110. Zatvoreno zbog odmora. *ZAT-vo-re-no zbog OD-mo-ra.* Closed for vacation.

2111. Zauzeto. *ZA-oo-ze-to.* Engaged (OR: Occupied).

2112. Za žene. *za ZHE-ne.* Ladies (OR: Ladies' room).

2113. Zoološki vrt. *zo-O-lo-shkee vŭrt.* Zoo.

2114. Zvoni. *ZVO-nee.* Ring the bell.

2115. Železnička stanica. *ZHE-le-zhneech-ka STA-nee-tsa.* Railroad station.

INDEX

The sentences, words and phrases in this book are numbered consecutively from 1 to 2115. The entries in the index refer to these numbers. In addition, each major section heading (capitalized entries) is indexed according to page number. In cases where the English entry is ambiguous, its part of speech is indicated by one of the following abbreviations: *adj.* for adjective, *adv.* for adverb, *n.* for noun, *prep.* for preposition and *v.* for verb. Parentheses are used for explanations, as they are in the body of the phrasebook. Eastern vocabulary variants are preceded in the index by (E); Western vocabulary variants by (W).

Because of the large volume of material indexed, cross-indexing has generally been avoided. Phrases or groups of words will usually be found under only one of their components, e.g., 'bathing suit" appears only under "bathing" even though there is a separate entry for "suit" alone. If you do not find a phrase under one word, try another.

Every English word or phrase in the index is followed by one or more Serbo-Croatian equivalents, which are ordinarily given in the standard dictionary form: the nominative singular for nouns, the indefinite masculine form for adjectives and the infinitive for verbs.

In effect, the reader is provided with an up-to-date English–Serbo-Croatian glossary. Of course, knowledge of Serbo-Croatian grammar is necessary for making the best use of this index, especially since Serbo-Croatian is an inflected language. To assist you in using the correct forms of words, the index lists all the sentences that contain different forms of a given word. For example, under "forget" (infinitive *zaboraviti*), sentences 146 and 188 are listed . They provide the forms *zaboravili* (past masculine plural) and *zaboravite* (imperative), respectively. Invariable forms are indexed only once, and only one appearance of each different variation is listed, so that there are no duplicate listings. The beginner would do well to look at all the sentences listed for a Serbo-Croatian word in order to become familiar with the possible range of variations (and at all the Serbo-Croatian equivalents listed for an English word in order to become familiar with their different shades of meaning).

It is not the purpose of the present book to teach Serbo-Croatian grammar, but it will give you the proper form to look up in a dictionary, where you will find more information.

Where a numbered sentence contains a choice of Serbo-Croatian equivalents (e.g., entry 259, which gives both *gimnastička sala* and *vežbaonica* for "gymnasium," only the first choice has been included in the index. Always refer to the numbered sentence for more information.

big: *veliki* 1226
bill(banknote): *novčanica* 1185; (check): *račun* 641, 815; (handbill) *plakata* 2100; (*v.*): *stavite na račun* 539
billion: *milijarda* 1964
birthday: *rodjendan* 1904
bite, insect: *ubod insekta* 1714
black: *crn* 185, 843, 1319
blanket: *ćebe* 653
bleed: *krvariti* 1773
blister: *plik* 1715
block (street): *blok* 223
blood: *krv* 1785; — pressure: *pritisak* 1668; — vessel: *krvni sud* 1786
blouse: *bluza* 1265, 1518
blue: *plav* 1320
board, go on: *ukrcati se* 245
boarding; — house: *pansion* 561; — pass: *bording karta* 294
BOAT, p. 19
body: *telo* 1787
boil (*n.*): *čir* 1716
boiled: *kuvan* 784, 959
bolt: *gvozden klin* 431
bone: *kost* 1788
bon voyage: *srećan put* 246
book (*n.*): *knjiga* 1357; (*v.*) *rezervisati* 1024
bookshop: *knjižara* 1591
BOOKSHOP, STATIONER, NEWSDEALER, p. 99
boot: *čizma* 1267
bored: *dosadno* 1056
boric acid: *borna kiselina* 1405
borrow: *pozajmiti* 403
botanical: *botanički* 1050
bottle: *flaša* 714, 1660; — opener: *otvarač za flaše* 677
boulevard: *bulevar* 219
bowel: *crevo* 1789
box: *kutija* 1489; (theater): *loža* 1089; — office: *blagajna* 1100
boy: *dečak* 76
boyfriend: *dečko* 53
bracelet: *narukvica* 1268
brains (food): *mozak* 901

cabin: *kabina* 257; — : stewart: *stjuard* 263
cablegram: *telegram pismo* 527
CAFÉ AND BAR, p. 56
cake: *kolač* 1010; *torta* 1021
calf (of leg): *list* 1792
call (*n.*): *poziv* 553; (= conversation): *razgovor* 536; (*v.*): *nazvati* 534; *pozvati* 341; *zvati* 288, 556, 634
camera: *foto-aparat* 1471
CAMERA SHOP AND PHOTOGRAPHY, p. 106
campsite: *kamping* 1160
can (*aux. v.*): *moći* 140, 248, 303; (= be allowed): *smeti* 1688
cancel: *otkazati* 265
candle: *sveća* 656
candy: box of — : *kutija bombona* 1489; — shop: *prodavnica bombona* 1593
cane: *štap* 1272
canned: *iz konzerve* 773
can opener: *otvarač za konzerve* 679
cantaloupe: *dinja* 987
cap: *kapa* 1273
captain: *kapetan* 261
car: *auto* 424; *kola* 359
carbon paper: *indigo* 1372
carburetor: *karburator* 436
card: *karta* 1136
careful, be: *biti pažljiv* 33
carefully: *pažljivo* 194, 350
carriage (baby): *kolica* 1655
carrot: (E): *šargarepa* 978; (W): *mrkva* 966
carry: *poneti* 189, 282; (= away): *odneti* 187
cash (*v.*): *unovčiti* 1181
cashier: *blagajnik* 642
cashier's desk: *blagajna* 813
castle: *zamak* 1047
cathedral: *katedrala* 1043
Catholic: *katolički* 1065
catsup: *kečap* 820
cauliflower: *karfiol* 955
cavity (= rotten tooth): *pokvaren zub* 1762

celery: *celer* 950
cemetery: *groblje* 2021
center: *centar* 202, 562
ceramic: *keramika* 1348
cereal (cooked): *kuvane žitne pahuljice* 866; (dry): *suve žitne pahuljice* 866
chain: *lanac* 492
chair: *stolica* 680
CHAMBERMAID, p. 51
chambermaid: *sobarica* 615, 625
champagne: *šampanjac* 735
change (*n.*): *sitnina* 356, 1186; (*v.*): *promeniti* 404; (= transfer): *menjati* 334
charge (*n.*): *tarifa* 529; (*v.*): *naplaćivati* 343; — additional (= pay additional) *doplatiti* 1259; cover — : *konzumacija* 1121; what is the — : *koliko košta* 537
chassis: *šasija* 437
cheap: *jevtin* 1201
cheaper: *jevtiniji* 599
check (*n.*): *ček* 1181, 1249; (bill): *račun* 812; (*v.*): *proveriti* 410; (baggage): *predati* 179; — in: *prijaviti se* 271; — out: *odjaviti se* 639
checkers: *dame* 1142
checkroom: *garderoba* 1594
cheek: *obraz* 1793
cheese: *sir* 860; — pie: *gibanica* 836
cherry: *trešnja* 1006
chess: *šah* 1141
chest of drawers: *orman* 681
chewing gum: *guma za žvakanje* 1406
chicken: *piletina* 875, 924; — pox: *srednje boginje* 1719; — soup: *pileća čorba* 872
children: *deca* 2008
chill: *drhtavica* 1720
chin: *brada* 1794
china: *kineski porculan* 1349

eraser: *guma za brisanje* 1361
escalator: *pokretne stepenice* 236
evening: *veče* 4; in the —: *uveče* 1864; this —: *večeras* 1086
event (=): *priredba* 1115
every: *svaki* 1663, 1868
EVERYDAY PHRASES, p. 1
everyone: *svi* 1098
everything: *sve* 169
exactly: *tačno* 1852
excellent: *odličan* 817
except (*prep.*): *osim* 2104
excess (weight): *višak* 281
exchange (*v.*): *razmeniti* 1183; *zameniti* 810, 1262
excursion: *izlet* 1023
excuse me: *izvinite* 14
exhaust pipe: *auspuh* 446
exit: *izlaz* 285, 1058
expect: *očekivati* 631
expensive: *skup* 1200
explain: *objasniti* 369
export: *izvoz* 1254
expressway: *autoput* 390
exterior (*n.*): *spoljašnost* 447
external: *spoljni* 1395
extract (*v.*): *izvaditi* 1764
eye: *oko* 1669; — wash: *kapi za oči* 1423
eyebrow: *obrva* 1563
eyelashes: *trepavice* 1799
eyelid: *očni kapak* 1800

face: *lice* 1445; — powder: *puder za lice* 1445
facial (*n.*): *masaža lica* 1575
factory: (E): *fabrika* 238; (W): *tvornica* 2085
faint (*v.*): *onesvestiti se* 1771
faint, I feel: *hvata me nesvestica* 1730
fair (weather): *lepo* 1883
fall (*v.*): *pasti* 1770
familiar: *poznati* 368
FAMILY, p. 141
fan (*n.*): *ventilator* 448; — belt: *remen za ventilator* 449
far: *daleko* 70
fare (= ticket): *karta* 329

prune: *suva šljiva* 1004
public (*adj.*): *javan* 2028
pudding: *puding* 1017
pull: *vući* 2095
puppet show: *predstava u pozorištu lutaka* 1113
purple: *ljubičast* 1327
purser: *blagajnik* 262
push: *gurati* 2022; *odgurati* 401; *pogurati* 402

QUANTITIES, p. 141
quarter: *četvrt* 1855; one — : *četvrtina* 1981
quickly: as — as you can: *što pre* 755
quiet: *tih* 563, 575; (= silence): *tišina* 2082

rabbi: *rabin* 1077
radiator: *radijator* 412; (car): *hladnjak* 485
radio: *radio* 486
rag: *krpa* 487
railroad station: *železnička stanica* 320
rain (*n.*): *kiša* 1881
raincoat: *kišni mantil* 1294
rare (meat): *nedopečen* 796
raspberry: *malina* 996
rate: *kurs* 1179, 1180; what is the — : *koliko košta* 528
rattle: *zvečka* 1664
razor (electric): *električni brijač* 1449; (straight): *običan brijač* 1449; — blade: *žilet* 1450
reach (arrive at): *stići* 530
read: *čitati* 120
ready: *gotov* 1233; get — : *spremiti* 615
real estate (office): *nekretnine* 1631
rear (*adj.*): *zadnji* 232, 507
reasonable (in price): *razumno* 1202
receipt: *potvrda* 184; *priznanica* 1256
recharge: *napuniti* 413
recommend: *preporučiti* 739, 1754
record, phonograph: *gramofonska ploča* 1497
red: *crven* 1328
reference: *podatak* 1251

well (adv.): *dobro* 39; — done (meat): *dobro pečeno* 798
west: *zapad* 207
what: *šta* 43; — for: *zašto* 816
wheel: *točak* 507
when: *kada* 60
where: *gde* 65; — to: *kuda* 380
which: *koji* 208, 1506
while, for a: *na kratko* 387
whisk broom: *četkica* 711
whiskey: *viski* 715
white: *beo* 838, 1330
who: *ko* 74, 545
whole (*n.*): *celina* 1985
wholesale: *prodaja na veliko* 2067
why: *zašto* 67
width: *širina* 1230
wife: *žena* 1989
wig: *perika* 1573
will (*v.*): *hteti* 532, 1682, 1689
window: *prozor* 284, 309; *šalter* 511; (store): *izlog* 1187
windshield: *šoferšajbna* 414; *vetrobran* 418; — wiper: *brisač* 508
windy: *vetrovito* 1885
wine: *vino* 736, 1647; — list: *vinska karta* 757; red — : *crno vino* 736; white — : *belo vino* 736
winter: *zima* 1923
with: *sa* 24
without: *bez* 772
woman: *žena* 81
wood: *drvo* 1356
wool: *vuna* 1347
word: *reč* 132
work (*v.*, = function): *raditi* 73, 423, 645
worse: *gore* 1685
WORSHIP, p. 79
wrap (*v.*): *spakovati* 1245
wrapping paper: *papir za pakovanje* 1383
wrench: *francuski ključ* 509
wrist: *ručni zglavak* 1850
write down: *zapisati* 128
writing paper: *hartija za pisanje* 1374

APPENDIX: COMMON ROAD SIGNS

Opasna krivina.
Dangerous bend.

Desna krivina.
Right bend.

Raskrsnica.
Intersection.

Rampa (OR: **Prelaz pruge).**
Level-crossing.

Otvoren prelaz pruge.
Level-crossing without gates.

Saobraćajni znakovi napred.
Traffic signals ahead.

Radovi na putu (W: **cesti**).
Road works.

Prelaz za pešake.
Pedestrian crossing.

Pazi škola.
Children (OR: School Crossing).

Pazi životinje.
Animal crossing.

Pazi suženje.
Road narrows.

Neravan put (OR: **Džombe).**
Uneven or rough road.

Pazi strmina.
Steep or dangerous hill.

Pazi klizav put.
Slippery road.

Prednost.
Right of way.

Dvosmerna ulica.
Two-way traffic ahead.

Opasnost.
Danger.

Pazi odron.
Danger from falling rock.

Stani pred raskrsnicom.
Stop at intersection.

Zabranjeno za sva vozila.
Closed to all vehicles.

Zabranjen pravac (OR: **smer).**
No entry.

Nema prolaza.
Dead end.

Ne skreći ulevo.
No left turns.

Zabranjen pun zaokret.
No U turns.

Zabranjeno preticanje.
No passing.

Maksimalna brzina.
Speed limit.

Ne trubi.
Sounding horn prohibited.

Zabranjeno parkiranje.
No parking.

Zabranjeno zaustavljanje.
Stopping prohibited.

Jedan smer.
One-way traffic.

Dvostruka krivina, prva ulica levo.
Double curve, first to the left.

Saobraćajna zvezda.
Traffic circle.